Berlitz®

P9-COP-231

Japanese
phrase book & dictionary

¥800

¥1250

50

¥1250

Berlitz Publishing
New York   London   Singapore

Contacting the Editors

Every effort has been made to provide accurate information in this publication, but changes are inevitable. The publisher cannot be responsible for any resulting loss, inconvenience or injury. We would appreciate it if readers would call our attention to any errors or outdated information. We also welcome your suggestions; if you come across a relevant expression not in our phrase book, please contact us at: **comments@berlitzpublishing.com**

All Rights Reserved
© 2007 Berlitz Publishing/APA Publications (UK) Ltd.
Berlitz Trademark Reg. U.S. Patent Office and other countries. Marca Registrada. Used under license from Berlitz Investment Corporation.

Eleventh Printing: March 2012
Printed in China

Publishing Director: Mina Patria
Commissioning Editor: Kate Drynan
Editorial Assistant: Sophie Cooper
Translation: updated by Wordbank
Cover Design: Beverley Speight
Interior Design: Beverley Speight
Production Manager: Raj Trivedi
Picture Researcher: Beverley Speight
Cover Photo: APA Ming Tang Evans and Istockphoto

Interior Photos: APA Ming Tnag Evans 1, 14, 16, 19, 23, 25, 28, 50, 53, 54, 56, 68, 70, 80, 82, 86, 92, 94, 96, 100, 132, 134, 137, APA Britta Jaschinski 85, APA Greg Gladman 90, Istockphoto 139, 140, APA Lucy Johnston 162

Contents

Food & Drink

People

Leisure Time

Special Requirements

In an Emergency

Dictionary

Pronunciation

This section is designed to familiarize you with the sounds of Japanese using simplified phonetic transcription. The pronunciation of the Japanese sounds is explained below, together with their 'imitated' equivalents. This system is used throughout the phrase book. When you see a word spelled phonetically, simply read the pronunciation as if it were English, noting any special rules.

Japanese is a unique language. Apart from a similarity of script (the Japanese adopted Chinese ideograms) it bears no resemblance to Chinese or other Asian languages, except for Korean. Where Japanese comes from is still a matter of conjecture. Japan, its people, customs, and language were almost totally isolated until the late nineteenth century.

Today there are many foreign 'loan' words that have been adopted into Japanese. From **pan** (from the Portuguese for bread) to **sportsman**, you will come across many foreign words, the majority of which are from English. At first hearing, you may not recognize these words because of the change in pronunciation and, conversely, you may not be understood when using a 'loan' word until you give it a Japanese pronunciation.

Japanese is composed less of vowels and consonants than of syllables, consisting of a consonant and a vowel. Consonants are always followed by vowels, except for **n**, which can occur alone. All syllables are pronounced with equal force: there is no stress except for emphasis.

Consonants

Letter	Approximate Pronunciation	Symbol	Example	Pronunciation
b	approximately as in English	**b**	バス	*basu*
ch	approximately as in English	**ch**	お茶	*ocha*
d	approximately	**d**	電車	*densha*

Letter	Approximate Pronunciation	Symbol	Example	Pronunciation
	as in English			
g	approximately as in English	d	外国	*gaikoku*
h	approximately as in English	h	箱根	*hakone*
j	approximately as in English	j	原宿	*harajuku*
k	approximately as in English	k	観光	*kankoo*
m	approximately as in English	m	鎌倉	*kamakura*
p	approximately as in English	p	乾杯	*kanpai*
s	approximately as in English	s	寿司	*sushi*
t	approximately as in English	t	成田	*narita*

Letter	Approximate Pronunciation	Symbol	Example	Pronunciation
f	with lips flattened and without putting lower teeth against lower lip, between an f and an h	f	お風呂	*ofuro*
n	1.before vowels like n in now	n	長い	*nagai*
	2. at the end	n	さん	*san*

	of a word, said without letting your tongue touch the roof of your mouth			
r	with tip of tongue against the gum behind the upper front teeth, between an r and an 1	**r**	りんご	*ringo*
w [semi-vowel]	the lips are not rounded but left slack	**w**	分かる	*wakaru*

Letter	Approximate Pronunciation	Symbol	Example	Pronunciation
z	1.at the beginning of words, like ds in beds	**z**	ゼロ	*zero*
	2. In the middle of words like z in zoo	**z**	水	*mizu*

Double consonants should be pronounced 'long', i.e. hold the sound for a moment. The doubling of a consonant is important as it can change the meaning of a word.

kk	一個	*ikko*
pp	かっぱ	*kappa*
tt	ちょっと	*chotto*

Vowels

Letter	Approximate Pronunciation	Symbol	Example	Pronunciation
A	like the a in father, Pronounced forward in the mouth	a	魚	*sakana*
e	like e in get	e	テレビ	*terebi*
i	like i in sit	i	イギリス	*igirisu*
o	like o in note	o	男	*otoko*
u	like u in put, but without rounding the lips	u	冬	*fuyu*

Long vowels (**aa**, **ee**, **ii**, **oo**, **uu**) are held for twice the amount of time. This is important in Japanese and can change the meaning of words, e.g. **oba(san)** means aunt while **obaa(san)** means grandmother.

Vowel clusters: when two vowels occur together (**ie, ai, ue, ao**) they should be pronounced separately with each vowel keeping its normal sound.

Consonant/double vowel clusters: (e.g. **kya, kyu, kyo**) these are two sounds said quickly so that they become one: **kya** is **ki** and **ya**.

Whispered vowels: sometimes **i** and **u** are devoiced, that is whispered or even omitted. This happens when **i** and **u** occur at the end of a word, or between voiceless consonants: **ch, f, h, k, p, s, sh, t,** and **ts**.

Japanese is composed of three different 'scripts' or ways of writing: **kanji** (Chinese characters or ideograms), **hiragana** (an alphabet in which each symbol represents a spoken syllable), and **katakana** (another alphabet). These three systems are used in combination to write modern Japanese.

Hiragana is used to link **kanji** characters together. **Katakana** is used to write foreign 'loan' words, most of which are English in origin.

In addition to these three 'scripts' you will find **romaji**, the Romanized system used to write Japanese. In Japan important signs and names are often given in **romaji**, for example the names of subway stations.

Traditionally Japanese is written from the top to the bottom of the page starting in the upper right-hand corner. Today it is also commonly written horizontally and from left to right. The Japanese phrases you will see in this book incorporate a mixture of **kanji**, **hiragana** and **katakana**, and the pronunciation is in **romaji**. Japanese words and phrases are pronounced very evenly, and stress is used only to emphasize meaning. Pitch does vary however; normal sentences will begin on a high note and finish on a low note.

As in English, questions normally rise in pitch at the end of the sentence.

How to use this Book

ESSENTIAL

Sometimes you see two alternatives separated by a slash. Choose the one that's right for your situation.

I'm here on vacation [holiday]/business.　観光/仕事で来ました。 *kankoo/ shigoto de kimashita*

I'm going to　...へ行きます。 *...e ikimasu*

I'm staying at the...
Hotel.　...ホテルに泊まっています *...hoteru ni tomatte imasu*

YOU MAY SEE...

Words you may see are shown in YOU MAY SEE boxes.

税関検査 *zeekan kensa*	customs
免税品 *menzeehin*	duty-free goods
課税 *kazee*	goods to declare

Any of the words or phrases listed can be plugged into the sentence below.

Winter Sports

A lift pass for a day/
five days please.　一日/五日 分のリフト券、お願いします。
ichinichi/itsuka bun no rifutoken onegai shimasu

I want to rent [hire]...　...を借りたいんですが 。 *...o karitain desu ga*

boots　スキー 靴 *sukii gutsu*

a helmet　ヘノレメット *herumetto*

poles　ストック *sutokku*

Japanese phrases appear in purple.

Read the simplified pronunciation as if it were English. For more on pronunciation, see page 7.

Personal

I'm	私は ...*watashi wa*
single	ひとりです。*hitoi desu*
in a relationship	付き合っています。*tsukiatte imasu*
married	結婚しています。*kekkon shite imasu*
divorced	離婚しました。*rikon shimashita*
separated	別居中です。*bekkyo chuu desu*
I'm widowed	妻/夫を亡くしました。*tsuma f / otto m o nakushimashita*

Related phrases can be found by going to the page number indicated.

When different gender forms apply, the masculine form is followed by *m*; feminine by *f*

Japan's rail network covers the whole country. There are many different rail operators, but the service is clean, safe, and punctual. First-class cars are called **guriin sha** (green cars) and are marked with a green four-leaf sign.

Information boxes contain relevant country, culture and language tips.

Expressions you may hear are shown in You May Hear boxes.

YOU MAY HEAR...

英語が少ししかできません。*eego ga sukoshi shika dekimasen*	I only speak a little English.
英語はできません。*eego wa dekimasen*	I don't speak English.

Color-coded side bars identify each section of the book.

Survival

Arrival & Departure

ESSENTIAL

I'm here on vacation [holiday]/business.	観光/仕事で来ました。 *kankoo/shigoto de kimashita*
I'm going to...	...へ行きます。 *...e ikimasu*
I'm staying at the... Hotel.	...ホテルに泊まっています。 *...hoteru ni tomatte imasu*

YOU MAY HEAR...

チケット/パスポートをお見せください。 *chiketto/pasupooto o omise kudasai*	Your ticket/ passport, please.
今回の旅行の目的は何ですか。 *konkai no ryokoo no mokuteki wa nan desu ka*	What's the purpose of your visit?
どこにお泊まりですか。 *doko ni otomari desu ka*	Where are you staying?
後、どのくらいいらっしゃいますか。 *ato donokurai irasshaimasu ka*	How long are you staying?
どなたとご一緒ですか。 *donata to goissho desu ka*	Who are you with?

Border Control

I'm just passing through.	立ち寄るだけです。 *tachiyoru dake desu*
I would like to declare...	...を申告します。 *...o shinkoku shimasu*
I have nothing to declare.	申告するものはありません。 *shinkoku suru mono wa arimasen*

YOU MAY HEAR...

申告するものはありますか。
shinkoku suru mono wa arimasu ka
関税がかかります。 *kanzee ga kakarimasu*
このバッグを開けてください。
kono baggu o akete kudasai

Do you have
anything to declare?
You must pay duty on this.
Please open this
bag.

YOU MAY SEE...

税関検査 *zeekan kensa*	customs
免税品 *menzeehin*	duty-free goods
課税 *kazee*	goods to declare
免税 *menzee*	nothing to declare
入国手続き *nyuukoku tetsuzuki*	passport control
警察 *keesatsu*	police

Money

ESSENTIAL

Where's...?	...はどこですか。...wa doko desu ka
the ATM	キャッシュコーナー kyasshu koonaa
the bank	銀行 ginkoo
the currency exchange office	両替所 ryoogaejo
What time does the bank open/close?	銀行は何時から/までですか。 ginkoo wa nanji kara/made desu ka
I'd like to change dollars/pounds to yen	ル/ポンドを円に替えたいんですが 。 doru/pondo o en ni kaetain desu ga
I want to cash some traveler's checks [cheques].	トラベラーズチェックを換金したいんですが。 toraberaazu chekku o kankin shitain desu ga

At the Bank

Can I exchange foreign currency here?	外国通貨の両替はできますか。 gaikoku tsuuka no ryoogae wa dekimasu ka
What's the exchange rate?	為替レートはいくらですか。 kawase reeto wa ikura desu ka
How much is the fee?	手数料はいくらですか。 tesuuryoo wa ikura desu ka
I've lost my traveler's checks [cheques].	トラベラーズチェックをなくしました。 toraberaazu chekku o nakushimashita

YOU MAY SEE...

The monetary system is the yen (円), abbreviated to ¥.
Coins: ¥1, ¥5, ¥10, ¥50, ¥100, and ¥500
Notes: ¥1,000, ¥2,000, ¥5,000, and ¥10,000

YOU MAY SEE...

カードを入れる	insert card
キャンセルする	cancel
消去する	clear
入力する	enter
暗証番号	PIN
引き出す	withdraw funds
当座預金口座から	from checking [current] account
普通預金口座から	from savings account
レシート/領収書	receipt

My card was lost.	カードをなくしました。 *kaado o nakushimashita*
My credit cards have been stolen.	クレジットカードを盗まれました。 *kurejitto kaado o nusumaremashita*
My card doesn't work.	カードが使えません。 *kaado ga tsukaemasen*

Banks are open from 9:00 a.m. to 5:00 p.m. Monday through Friday. Some banks are open on Saturdays and all banks are closed on Sundays, except the bank at Tokyo Airport, which is open 24 hours a day. Most banks have a foreign currency section. You will need to show your passport to change foreign currency or traveler's checks. You will usually be invited to sit down while the transaction is conducted, which may take as long as 15 minutes. Your name will be called when your money is ready. You will not be able to use foreign credit cards to get cash from most ATMs, except those run by Citibank (the only foreign bank currently operating in Japan) and the Postal Service. Every post office in Japan has an ATM where you can obtain cash using international credit cards or cash cards from your bank. In rural areas the banks may not have currency exchange facilities. The safest solution is to have cash with you at all times.

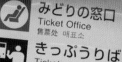

Getting Around

ESSENTIAL

How do I get to town?	どうしたら町に行けますか。 *dooshitara machi ni ikemasu ka*
How far is it?	距離はどのくらいですか。 *kyori wa dono kurai desu ka*
Where can I buy tickets?	切符はどこで買えますか。 *kippu wa doko de kaemasu ka*
Where's…?	…はどこですか。 *…wa doko desu ka*
the airport	空港 *kuukoo*
the train station	駅 *eki*
the bus station	バスターミナル *basu taaminaru*
the subway [underground] station	地下鉄の駅 *chikatetsu no eki*
A one-way [single]/round-trip [return] ticket.	片道/往復 *katamichi/oofuku*
How much?	いくらですか。 *ikura desuka*

Are there any discounts?	割引料金はありますか。 *waribiki ryookin wa arimasu ka*
Which…?	どちらの… *dochira no…*
gate	ゲート *geeto*
line	線 *sen*
platform	ホーム *hoomu*
Where can I get a taxi?	タクシーはどこで乗れますか。 *takushii wa doko de noremasu ka*
Please take me to this address.	この住所までお願いします。 *konojuusho made onegai shimasu*
Where can I rent a car?	レンタカーはどこで借りられますか。 *rentakaa wa doko de kariraremasu ka*
Can I have a map?	地図をお願いします。 *chizu o onegai shimasu*

Tickets

When's…to Kyoto?	京都行きの…は何時ですか。 *kyootoikino…wa nanji desu ka*
the (first) bus	(始発)バス *(shihatsu) basu*
the (next) flight	(次の)便 *(tsugi no) bin*
the last train	終電 *shuuden*
Where can I buy tickets?	切符はどこで買えますか。 *kippu wa doko de kaemasu ka*
One/Two ticket(s), please.	切符一枚/二枚 お願いします。 *kippu ichimai/nimai onegai shimasu*
For today/tomorrow.	今日/あした の *kyoo/ashita no*
A…ticket	…チケット …*chiketto*
one-way [single]	片道 *katamichi*
round-trip [return]	往復 *oofuku*
first class	ファーストクラス *faasuto kurasu*

business class	ビジネス・クラス *bijinesu kurasu*
economy class	エコノミー *ekonomii*
How much?	いくらですか。*ikura desuka*
Is there a discount for…?	…割引はありますか。…*waribiki wa arimasu ka*
children	子供の *kodomo no*
students	学生 *gakusee*
senior citizens	高齢者 *kooreesha*
tourists	観光客向けの *kankookyaku mukeno*
The express bus/express train, please.	高速バス/特急電車をお願いします。*koosoku basu / tokkyuu densha o onegai shimasu*
The local bus/train, please.	路線バス/普通電車をお願いします。*rosen basu / futsuu densha o onegai shimasu*
I have an e-ticket.	Eチケットがあります。*iichiketto ga arimasu*
Can I buy a ticket on the bus/train?	バス/電車の中で切符が買えますか。*basu/densha no nakade kippu ga kaemasu ka*
I'd like to…my reservation.	予約を…したいんですが。*yoyaku o …shitian desu ga*
cancel	キャンセル *kyanseru*
change	変更 *henkoo*
confirm	確認 *kakunin*

For Days, see page 159.

For Time, see page 158.

Plane

Airport Transfer

How much is a taxi to the airport?	空港までタクシーはいくらですか。*kuukoo made takushii wa ikura desu ka*
To…Airport, please.	…空港までお願いします。*…kuukoo made onegai shimasu*
My airline is…	航空会社は…です。*kookuu gaisha wa…desu*

My flight leaves at...	飛行機の便は...に出ます。
	hikooki no bin wa... ni demasu
I'm in a rush.	急いでいます。*isoide imasu*
Can you take an	他の道を行ってください。
alternate route?	*hoka no michi o itte kudasai*
Can you drive faster/	もっと はやく/ ゆっくり
slower?	運転してくれませんか。*motto hayaku/*
	yukkuri unten shite kuremasenka

YOU MAY HEAR...

どの航空会社をご利用ですか。	What airline are
dono kookuu gaisha o goriyoo desu ka	you flying?
国内線ですか,国際線ですか。	Domestic or
kokunaisen desu ka kokusaisen desu ka	International?
どのターミナルですか。	What terminal?
dono taaminaru desu ka	

YOU MAY SEE...

到着 *toochaku*	arrivals
出発 *shuppatsu*	departures
荷物引渡場 *nimotsu hikiwatashijoo*	baggage claim
国内線 *kokunaisen*	domestic flights
国際線 *kokusaisen*	international flights
チェックインデスク *chekku in desuku*	check-in desk
Eチケットチェックイン *e-chiketto chekku in*	e-ticket check-in
出発ゲート *shuppatsu geeto*	departure gates

Checking In

Where is the check-in desk for flight…?	…便のチェックインデスクはどこですか。 *…bin no chekkuin desuku wa doko desu ka*
My name is…	…です。*…desu*
I'm going to…	…へ行きます。*…e ikimasu*
How much luggage is allowed?	荷物はどれくらい持ち込めますか。 *nimotsu wa dore kurai mochikomemasu ka*
Which gate does flight… leave from?	…便のゲートは何番ですか。 *…bin no geeto wa nanban desu ka*
I'd like a window/an aisle seat.	窓側/通路側 の席をお願いします。 *madogawa/tsuurogawa no seki o onegaishimasu*
When do we leave/ arrive?	何時に出ますか/着きますか。 *nanji ni demasu ka/tsukimasu ka*
Is flight…delayed?	…便は遅れていますか。*…bin wa okurete imasu ka*
How late will it be?	どのくらい遅れますか。*dono kurai okuremasu ka*

YOU MAY HEAR...

次の方 *tsugi no kata* — Next!

チケット/パスポートをお見せください。
chiketto/pasupooto o omise kudasai — Your ticket/ passport, please.

お荷物はいくつありますか。
onimotsu wa ikutsu arimasu ka — How many pieces of luggage do you have?

重量超過です。*juuryoo chooka desu* — You have excess baggage.

それは手荷物には重すぎます/
大きすぎます。*sore wa tenimostu ni wa omosugimasu/ookisugimasu* — That's too heavy/large for a carry-on [to carry on board].

お荷物は、ご自分で詰められましたか。
onimotsu wa gojibun de tsumeraremashita ka — Did you pack these bags yourself?

誰かに何か運ぶように頼まれましたか。
dareka ni nanika hakobuyooni tanomaremashita ka — Did anyone give you anything to carry?

ポケットのものを出してください。
poketto no mono o dashite kudasai — Empty your pockets.

靴を脱いでください。*kutsu o nuide kudasai* — Take off your shoes.

...便のお客様はご搭乗いただきます。
...bin no okyakusama wa gotoojoo itadakimasu — Now boarding flight...

Luggage

Where is/are the...?	...はどこですか。*...wa doko desu ka*
luggage carts [trolleys]	カート *kaato*
luggage lockers	コインロッカー *koin rokkaa*
baggage claim	荷物引渡場 *nimotsu hikiwatashijoo*
My luggage has been lost.	荷物がなくなりました。 *nimotsu ga nakunarimashita*

A Travel Help Line is run by the Japan National Tourist Organization (JNTO). An English-speaking travel expert is available. Ask at your hotel or at a tourist information center for the phone number.

My luggage has been stolen.	荷物が盗まれました。	*nimotsu ga nusumaremashita*
My suitcase was damaged.	スーツケースが壊れています。	*suutsukeesu ga kowarete imasu*

Finding your Way

Where is/are the...?	...はどこですか。	*...wa doko desu ka*
currency exchange office	両替所	*ryoogaejo*
car rental [hire]	レンタカー	*rentakaa*
Where is/are the...?	...はどこですか。	*...wa doko desu ka*
exit	出口	*deguchi*
taxis	タクシー	*takushii*
Is there a...into town?	町に行く...はありますか。	*machi ni iku...wa arimasu ka*
bus	バス	*basu*

電車 *densha*
地下鉄 *chikatetsu*

king Directions, see page 35.

Train

How do I get to the train station?	駅には、どうやって行けますか。 *eki niwa doo yatte ikemasu ka*
How far is it?	距離はどのくらいですか。 *kyori wa dono kurai desu ka*
Where is/are the...?	...はどこですか。 *...wa doko desu ka*
ticket office	きっぷうりば *kippu uriba*
information desk	受付 *uketsuke*
luggage lockers	コインロッカー *koin rokkaa*
platforms	ホーム *hoomu*
Can I have a schedule [timetable]?	時刻表をください。 *jikokuhyoo o kudasai*
How long is the trip?	どのくらいかかりますか。 *dono kurai kakarimasu ka*
Is it a direct train?	この電車は直行便ですか。 *kono densha wa chokkoobin desu ka*
Do I have to change trains?	乗り換えはありますか。 *norikae wa arimasu ka*
Is the train on time?	電車は時間通りですか。 *densya wa jikandoori desu ka*

YOU MAY SEE...

ホーム	platforms
案内係	information
予約窓口	reservations
到着	arrivals
出発	departures

Japan's rail network covers the whole country. There are many different rail operators, and the service is clean, safe, and punctual. First-class cars are called **guriin sha** (green cars) and are marked with a green four-leaf sign. To travel first class you need a special ticket in addition to the normal ticket. Second-class cars have reserved seats and unreserved seats. Reserved seats are a little more expensive. The types of train are:

新幹線 **shinkansen**, the bullet train. This is the fastest rail service. There are lines in Honshu (main island), Kyushu (south island), and Hokkaido (north island). There are three types: **Nozomi** (the fastest train), **Hikari** and **Kodama**.

特急 **tokkyuu**, limited express. This service is for long-distance travel.

急行 **kyuuko**, the ordinary medium-distance express.

快速 **kaisoku**, rapid train. This commuter service has no surcharge above the basic fare.

普通 **futsuu**, local train. This commuter service has no surcharge above the basic fare.

Tourists can buy special passes for unlimited travel on the rail system, as well as on buses and ferries, throughout Japan. These passes must be bought outside Japan, from offices of Japan Air Lines, travel agents, or Japan Travel Bureau offices.

There are a number of other special discounts for travel along certain lines within designated areas over a set period, for example **Shuuyuuken** (周遊券), **Free kippu** (フリーきっぷ), and **Parent-Child Super Pass** (親子スーパーパス). Enquire about these tickets at station travel shops. Most tickets are bought from vending machines. Find your destination on the diagram above the machines, insert money (change is given), and press the button for the appropriate amount. The station names on the diagram are usually in Japanese only, so it is important to know the characters of the station you are going to.

Departures

Which track [platform] for the train to…?	…行きの列車は何番ホームですか。 *…iki no ressha wa nan-ban hoomu desu ka*
Is this the track [platform] to…?	…行きのホームはここですか。 *… iki no hoomu wa koko desu ka*
Where is track [platform]…?	…行きのホームはどこですか。 *… iki no hoomu wa doko desu ka*
Where do I change for…?	…へ行くには、どこで乗り換えますか。 *…e ikuniwa doko de norikaemasu ka*

YOU MAY HEAR…

ご乗車の方はお急ぎください。 *gojoosha no kata wa oisogi kudasai*	All aboard!
乗車券を拝見します。 *jooshaken o haiken shimasu*	Tickets, please.
…で乗り換えてください。 *…de norikaete kudasai*	You have to change at…
次の停車駅は…*tsugi no teishaeki wa …*	Next stop…

There are extensive city and rural bus services in Japan. Some
towns, such as Hakone, Nagasaki and Kumamoto, have streetcars
[trams]. When you board a bus take a numbered ticket and pay at the
end. You can save money by buying **kaisuuken**, multiple-ride tickets.

On Board

Can I sit here?	ここに座ってもいいですか。
	koko ni suwattemo iidesuka
Can I open the window?	窓を開けてもいいですか。
	mado o aketemo iidesu ka
Is this seat taken?	この席は空いていますか。
	kono seki wa aite imasu ka
That's my seat.	そこは私の席です。 *soko wa watashi no seki desu*
Here's my reservation.	こちらが予約票です。 *kochira ga yoyakuhyoo desu*

Bus

Where's the bus station?	バスのターミナルはどこですか。
	basu no taaminaru wa doko desu ka
How far is it?	距離はどのくらいですか。
	kyori wa dono kurai desu ka
How do I get to…?	どうしたら…に行けますか。
	dooshitara…ni ikemasu ka
Does the bus stop at…?	…に止まりますか。 *…ni tomarimasu ka*
Could you tell me when to get off?	下りる場所が来たら、教えてください。
	oriru basho ga kitara oshiete kudasai

YOU MAY SEE…

| バス停留所/バス停 | bus stop |
| 入口/出口 | enter/exit |

Tokyo, Osaka, Nagoya and other big cities have very efficient subway systems. A map showing the various lines and stations is displayed outside **chikatetsu**, subway stations. Trains are frequent and run until around midnight. Station platform signs are in Japanese and English. Avoid rush hours (7:00 - 9:00 a.m. and 5:00 - 7:00 p.m.), when trains can be extremely crowded.

Do I have to change buses?	乗り換えはありますか。 *norikae wa arimasu ka*
Stop here, please!	ここで止めてください。 *kokode tomete kudasai*

For Tickets, see page 20.

Subway

Where's the nearest Subway station?	最寄りの地下鉄の駅はどこですか。 *moyori no chikatetsu no eki wa doko desu ka*
Could I have a map of the subway, please?	地下鉄の路線図をください。 *chikatetsu no rosenzu o kudasai*
Which line for...?	...は、何線ですか。 *...wa nanisen desu ka*
Which direction?	どこ行きですか。 *doko iki desu ka*
Do I have to transfer [change]?	乗り換えが必要ですか。 *norikae ga hitsuyoo desu ka*
Is this the subway [train] to...?	この電車は...へ行きますか。 *kono densha wa...e ikimasu ka*
How many stops to...?	...までの停車駅はいくつですか。 *...made no teesya eki wa ikutsu desu ka*
Where are we?	ここは、どこですか。 *koko wa doko desu ka*

Boat & Ferry

When is the car ferry to Okinawa?	沖縄行きのカーフェリーは、何時ですか。 *okinawa iki no kaa ferii wa nanji desu ka*

YOU MAY SEE...

| 救命ボート | life boats |
| 救命ベルト | life jackets |

What time is the next sailing?	次の出航は何時ですか。
	tsugi no syukkoo wa nanji desu ka
Can I book a seat/ cabin?	座席/船室を予約したいんですが。
	zaseki / senshitsu o yoyaku shitain desu ga
How long is the crossing?	到着までどのくらいかかりますか。
	toochaku made dono kurai kakarimasu ka

For Tickets, see page 20.

Taxi

Where can I get a taxi?	タクシーはどこで乗れますか。
	takushii wa doko de noremasu ka
I'd like a taxi now/ for tomorrow.	今/ 明日 タクシーをお願いします。
	ima/ashita takushii o onegai shimasu
Do you have the number for a taxi?	タクシー会社の電話番号をご存知ですか。
	takushii gaisha no denwa bangoo o gozonji desu ka

Ferry services run from Honshu (the main island) to the other islands. Details about ports and sailings may be obtained from the Tourist Information Center (TIC). To sample the charms of the Inland Sea, travel by ferry or hydrofoil is recommended.

Various cruises are available in the Tokyo Bay area, many departing from Hinode Pier (日の出桟橋 **hinode sanbashi**). In Kobe, travelers may enjoy 50-minute port cruises departing from Naka Pier. In Yokohama, you can find 50-minute tours of the harbor leaving from near the retired cruise liner, Hikawa Maru.

Can you send a taxi?	タクシーを呼んでもらえますか。 *takushii o yonde morae masu ka*
Pick me up at (place/ time).	(place)に/(time)に来てください。 *. . . ni kite kudasai*
I'm going to. . .	. . .へ行きます。*. . . e ikimasu*
this address	この住所 *kono juusho*
the airport	空港 *kuukoo*
the train [railway] station	駅 *eki*
I'm late.	急いでいるんです。*isoide irun desu*
Can you drive faster/ slower?	急いで/ゆっくり運転してください。 *isoide/yukkuri unten shite kudasai*
Stop/Wait here.	ここで止めて/待っていてください。 *kokode tomete/matteite kudasai*
How much?	いくらですか。*ikura desuka*
You said it would cost. . .yen.	. . .円ですね。*. . . en desu ne*

Taxis are usually yellow or green. If the light in the bottom
right-hand corner of the windshield is red, the taxi is free; if it's
green, it's occupied. The rear doors are remote controlled — be
careful not to get knocked over by them! Few taxi drivers speak English,
so have your destination written down on paper. Taxi drivers do not
expect to be tipped.

| Keep the change. | お釣りは結構です。 *otsuri wa kekkoo desu* |
| A receipt, please. | レシートをお願いします。 *reshiito o onegai shimasu* |

Bicycle & Motorbike

I'd like to rent...	...を借りたいんですが。 ...*o karitain desu ga*
a 3-/10-speed bicycle	3速/10速 の自転車 *sansoku/jussoku no jitensha*
a moped	スクーター *sukuutaa*
a motorcycle	オートバイ *ootobai*
How much per day/ week?	一日/一週間、いくらですか。いくらですか。 *ichinichi/isshuukan ikura desu ka*
Can I have a helmet/ lock?	ヘルメット/ロックをお願いします。 *herumetto/rokku o onegai shimasu*
I have a puncture/ flat tyre.	タイヤがパンクしています。 *taiya ga panku shite imasu*

Car Hire

Where can I rent a car?	レンタカーはどこで借りられますか。 *rentakaa wa doko de kariraremasu ka*
I'd like to rent...	...を借りたいんですが。 ...*o karitain desu ga*
a 2-/4-door car	2/4ドア車 *tsuu/foo doa sha*
an automatic	オートマチック *ootomachikku*
a car with air conditioning	エアコン付の車 *eakon tsuki no kuruma*
a car seat	チャイルドシート *chairudo shiito*
How much...?	いくら *ikura*
per day/week	一日/一週間 *ichinichi/isshuukan*
per kilometer	一キロ *ichi kiro*
for unlimited mileage	距離は無制限で *kyori wa museigen de*
with insurance	保険付きで *hoken tsuki de*

国際免許証をお持ちですか。
kokusai menkyoshoo o omochi desu ka

Do you have an international driver's license?

パスポートをお見せください。
pasupooto o omise kudasai

Your passport, please.

保険をお掛けになりますか。
hoken o okakeni narimasu ka

Do you want insurance?

...の前金をいただきます。
...no maekin o itadakimasu

There is a deposit of...

ここにサインをお願いします。
koko ni sain o onegai shimasu

Please sign here.

Are there any special weekend rates?	週末料金はありますか。 *shuumatsu ryookin wa arimasu ka*
(Where's) the parking meter?	パーキングメーター（はどこですか。）*paakingu meetaa (wa doko desu ka)*
(Where's...) the parking garage?	駐車場（はどこですか。） *chuushajoo (wa doko desu ka)*

Fuel Station

Where's the fuel station?	ガソリンスタンドはどこですか。 *gasorin sutando wa doko desu ka*
Fill it up, please.	満タンにしてください。*mantan ni shite kudasai*
...liters, please.	...リットルお願いします。*...rittoru onegai shimasu*

YOU MAY SEE...

レギュラー	regular
スーパー	premium [super]
ディーゼル	diesel

| I'll pay in cash/by credit card. | 現金/(クレジット)カード で 払います。 |
| | *genkin/(kurejitto) kaado de haraimasu* |

Asking Directions

Is this the right road to...?	...に行くのは、この道でいいんですか。
	...ni ikuno wa kono michi de iin desu ka
How far is it to...?	...まで、どのくらいありますか。
	...made donokurai arimasu ka
Where's...?	...はどこですか。 *...wa doko desu ka*
...Street	...通り *...doori*
this address	この住所 *kono juusho*
the highway [motorway]	高速道路 *koosoku dooro*
Can you show me on the map?	この地図で教えてください。
	kono chizu de oshiete kudasai
I'm lost.	道に迷いました。 *michi ni mayoimashita*

YOU MAY HEAR...

まっすぐ *massugu*	straight ahead
左 *hidari*	left
右 *migi*	right
角/道を曲がったところ *kado/michi o magatta tokoro*	on/around the corner
向かい *mukai*	across
後ろ *ushiro*	behind
のとなり *no tonari*	next to
北/南 *kita/minami*	north/south
東/西 *higashi/nishi*	east/west
信号 *shingoo*	traffic light
交差点 *koosaten*	intersection

YOU MAY SEE...

 stop

 minimum speed

 no standing

 dangerous curve

 no entry

 slow down

 time limited parking

 no parking

 one way

Parking

Can I park here?	ここに駐車してもいいですか。
	koko ni chuusha shitemo ii desu ka
Where is the nearest parking garage?	この近くに駐車場はありますか。
	kono chikaku ni chuushajoo wa arimasu ka
How much...?	...いくらですか。 *...ikura desuka*
per hour	一時間 *ichijikan*
per day	一日 *ichinichi*
overnight	一晩 *hitoban*
(Where's) the parking meter?	パーキングメーター (はどこですか。)
	paakingu meetaa (wa doko desu ka)

Street parking is limited. It is common to have your car towed away or booted if you park in illegal spaces. It is an expensive and time-consuming process to get it back. Some hotels have parking facilities, otherwise the best solution is to use designated parking garages.

Breakdown & Repair

My car broke down/ won't start.	車が壊れました。/スタートしません。 *kuruma ga kowaremashita/sutaato shimasen*
Can you fix it?	直してもらえませんか。 *naoshite moraemasen ka*
When will it be ready?	いつ直りますか。 *itsu naorimasu ka*
How much?	いくらですか。 *ikura desuka*
I have a puncture/ flat tyre.	タイヤがパンクしています。 *taiya ga panku shite imasu*

Accidents

There has been an accident.	事故がありました。 *jiko ga arimashita*
Call an ambulance/ the police.	警察/救急車を呼んでください。 *keesatsu/ kyuukyuusha o yonde kudasai*

Places to Stay

ESSENTIAL

Can you recommend a hotel in...?	...で良いホテルを教えてください。 *...de ii hoteru o oshiete kudasai*
I have a reservation.	予約してあります。 *yoyaku shite arimasu*
My name is...	...です。 *...desu*
Do you have a room...?	...部屋はありますか。 *...heya wa arimasu ka*
with a bathroom	バス付きの *basu tsuki no*
with AC	エアコン付きの *eakon tsuki no*
Do you have a room for one/two?	一人/二人部屋はありますか。 *hitori/futari beya wa arimasuka*
For tonight	今晩 *konban*
For two nights	二晩 *futaban*

37

For one week	一週間 *isshuukan*
How much?	いくらですか。 *ikura desuka*
Is there anything cheaper?	もっと安い部屋はありますか。 *motto yasui heya wa arimasu ka*
When's check-out?	チェックアウトは何時ですか。 *chekkuautowa nanji desu ka*
Can I leave this in the safe?	これを金庫に預けたいんですが。 *kore o kinko ni azuketain desu ga*
Can I leave my bags?	荷物を預けたいんですが。 *nimotsu o azuketain desu ga*
Can I have the bill/a receipt?	レシート/会計 をお願いします。 *kaikee/reshiito o onegai shimasu*
I'll pay in cash/by credit card.	現金/(クレジット)カード で払います。 *genkin/(kurejitto) kaado de haraimasu*

Somewhere to Stay

Can you recommend a hotel?	いホテルを教えてください。 *iihoteruooshiete kudasai*
Can you recommend a capsule hotel?	どこか良いカプセルホテルはありますか。 *dokoka yoi kapuseru hoteru wa arimasu ka*
Can you recommend a hostel?	どこか良い ホステル はありますか 。 *dokoka yoi hosuteru wa arimasu ka*
Can you recommend a campsite?	どこか良い キャンプ場 はありますか 。 *dokoka yoi kyanpujoo wa arimasu ka*
Can you recommend a bed and breakfast?	どこか良い 民宿 はありますか 。 *dokoka yoi minsyuku wa arimasu ka*
Can you recommend an inn?	どこか良い 旅館 はありますか 。 *dokoka yoi ryokan wa arimasu ka*
What is it near?	どこの近くですか。 *doko no chikaku desu ka*
How do I get there?	どうやって行くんですか。 *dooyatte ikun desu ka*

A wide variety of accommodations are available in Japan. ホテル **hoteru** are Western-style hotels. These are comparable to western hotels.

ビジネスホテル **bijinesu hoteru**, or business hotels, have small rooms, often with no room service. They are clean and comfortable and usually located near train stations.

旅館 **ryokan** are Japanese-style inns. For a taste of the Japanese way of life, a stay at a **ryokan** is recommended. Many are situated in beautiful settings with access to hot springs. Room prices include breakfast, dinner, and service charge. The majority offer only traditional style bathrooms, meals and sleeping arrangements.

Another good way of sampling authentic Japanese lodgings is a 民宿 **minshuku**, or guest house. **Minshuku** are often family run and have an informal, friendly atmosphere. The overnight charge includes dinner and breakfast.

For those with a particular interest in Buddhism, 宿防 **shukuboo**, temple accommodation, will allow you to join in the monks' daily life.

At the Hotel

I have a reservation.	予約してあります。	*yoyaku shite arimasu*
My name is...	...です。	*...desu*
Do you have a room...?	...部屋はありますか。	*...heya wa arimasu ka*
with a bathroom [toilet]/shower	バス/シャワー付きの	*basu/shawaa tukino*
with AC	エアコンつきの	*eakon tsuki no*
that's smoking/ non-smoking	喫煙/禁煙の	*kitsuen/kinen no*
for tonight	今晩	*konban*
for two nights	二晩	*futaban*

for one week	一週間 *isshuukan*
Does the hotel have...?	ホテルに...はありますか。
	hoteru ni... wa arimasu ka
a computer	コンピュータ *konpyuuta*
an elevator [lift]	エレベーター *erebeetaa*
(wireless) internet service	(ワイアレス)インターネットサービス *(waiaresu) intaanetto saabisu*
room service	ルームサービス *ruumu saabisu*
a gym	フィットネスセンター *fittonesu sentaa*
a pool	プール *puuru*
I need...	...が要るんですが。 *...ga irun desu ga*
an extra bed	もう一つベッド *moo hitotsu beddo*
a cot	折り畳みベッド *oritatami beddo*
a crib [child's cot]	ベビーベッド *bebii beddo*

YOU MAY HEAR...

パスポート/カード をお願いします。
pasupooto/kaado o onegai shimasu
この用紙にご記入ください。
kono yooshi ni gokinyuu kudasai
ここにサインをお願いします。
koko ni sain o onegai shimasu

Your passport/credit card, please.
Please fill out this form.
Sign here.

Price

How much per night/ week?	一泊/一週間いくらですか。
	ippaku/isshuukan ikura desu ka
Does the price include breakfast/sales tax [VAT]?	この料金は朝食/消費税 込みですか。
	kono ryookin wa chooshoku/shoohi zee komi desu ka

Preferences

Can I see the room?	部屋を見せてもらえますか。
	heya o misete morae masu ka
I'd like a...room.	...部屋にしてもらえますか。
	...heya ni shite morae masu ka
better	もっと良い *motto yoi*
bigger	もっと大きい *motto ookii*
cheaper	もっと安い *motto yasui*
quieter	もっと静かな *motto shizuka na*
I'll take it.	それにします。 *sore ni shimasu*
No, I won't take it.	いいえ、結構です。 *Iie kekkou desu*

Questions

Where's the...?	...はどこですか。 *...wa doko desu ka*
bar	バー *baa*
bathroom [toilet]	トイレ *toire*
elevator [lift]	エレベーター *erebeetaa*
Can I have...?	...をお願いします。 *...o onegai shimasu*
a blanket	毛布 *moofu*
an iron	アイロン *airon*
the room key	ルームキー *ruumu kii*
key card	キーカード *kii kaado*
a pillow	枕 *makura*
soap	石鹸 *sekken*
toilet paper	トイレットペーパー *toiretto peepaa*
a towel	タオル *taoru*
Do you have an adapter for this?	アダプタはありますか。 *adaputa wa arimasu ka*
How do I turn on the lights?	電気はどうやって付けますか。
	denki wa dooyatte tsukemasu ka
Could you wake me at...?	...時に起こしてください。
	...ji ni okoshite kudasai

Can I leave this in the safe?	これを金庫に保管できますか。
	kore o kinko ni hokan dekimasu ka
Could I have my things from the safe?	私のものを金庫から出してください。
	watashi no mono o kinko kara dashite kudasai
Is/are there any mail/ messages for me?	手紙/メッセージがありますか。
	tegami/messeeji ga arimasu ka
Do you have a laundry service?	ランドリーサービスはありますか。
	randorii saabisu wa arimasu ka

There are two types of toilet you may find in Japan. Traditional Japanese squat toilets have nothing to sit down on, and the user squats down to use the facility. These toilets flush just like western style. You will also find some toilets like you see in the West. Western style toilets may range from very basic to a high-tech model which will have a heated seat, water jets to wash and warm air to dry, and an automatic mechanism to flush and close the lid.

YOU MAY SEE...

押す/引く	push/pull
トイレ	restroom [toilet]
シャワー	shower
エレベーター	elevator [lift]
階段	stairs
洗濯室	laundry
起こさないでください	do not disturb
防火扉	fire door
非常口	(emergency) exit
モーニングコール	wake-up call

Problems

There's a problem.	ちょっと困っているんですが。
	chotto komatte irun desu ga
I've lost my key/key card.	鍵/カードキー をなくしました。
	kagi/kaado kii o nakushimashita
I've locked myself out of my room.	鍵を部屋に置いたまま出てきてしまいました。
	kagi o heya ni oitamama detekite shimaimashita
There's no hot water/ toilet paper.	お湯/トイレットペーパーがないんですが。
	oyu/toiretto peepaa ga nain desuga
The room is dirty.	部屋が汚いんですが。 *heya ga kitanain desu ga*
There are bugs in our room.	部屋に虫がいるんですが。
	heya ni mushi ga irun desuga
The...has broken down.	...が壊れたんですが。 *...ga kowaretan desuga*
Can you fix...?	...を直してもらえますか。
	...o naoshite moraemasu ka
the AC	エアコン *eakon*
the fan	扇風機 *senpuuki*
the heat [heating]	暖房 *danboo*
the light	電気 *denki*
the TV	テレビ *terebi*
the toilet	トイレ *toire*
I'd like to move to another room.	部屋を替えてください。*heya o kaete kudasai*

Japan uses the 100 volt electricity system. You may need a converter and/or adapter for your appliances.

Checking Out

When's check-out?	チェックアウトは何時ですか。
	chekkuauto wa nanji desu ka
Could I leave my bags here until…?	…まで荷物を置いておいてもいいですか。
	…made nimotsu o oite oitemo ii desu ka
Can I have an itemized bill/a receipt?	明細書/レシート をお願いします。
	meesaisho/reshiito o onegai shimasu
I think there's a mistake in this bill.	この会計は違っているようですが。
	kono kaikee wa chigatte iru yoo desu ga
I'll pay in cash/by credit card.	現金/(クレジット)カードで払います。
	genkin/(kurejitto) kaado de haraimasu

Tipping isn't customary and is officially discouraged. Porters at airports and train stations charge a set fee. Hotels, **ryokan** (Japanese inns) and restaurants add a 10-15% service charge to the bill.

Renting

I've reserved an apartment/a room.	アパート/部屋 を借りました。
	apaato/heya o karimashita
My name is…	…です。*…desu*
Can I have the key/key card?	鍵/カードキー をお願いします。
	kagi/kaado kii o onegai shimasu
Are there…?	…はありますか *…wa arimasu ka*
dishes and utensils	食器 *shokki*
pillows	枕 *makura*
Are there…?	…はありますか 。*…wa arimasu ka*
sheets	シーツ *shiitsu*

towels	タオル	*taoru*
When/Where do I put out the trash [rubbish]?	ゴミはどこへ/いつ出すんですか。 *gomi wa doko e/itsu dasun desu ka*	
...is broken.	...が壊れているんですが。 *...ga kowarete irun desuga*	
How does...work?	...はどうやって使えばいいんですか。 *...wa dooyatte tsukaeba ii n desu ka*	
the air-conditioner	エアコン	*eakon*
the dishwasher	食洗機	*shokusen ki*
the freezer	冷凍庫	*reetooko*
the heater	ヒーター	*hiitaa*
the microwave	電子レンジ	*denshi renji*
the refrigerator	冷蔵庫	*reezooko*
the stove	コンロ	*konro*
the washing machine	洗濯機	*sentakuki*

Domestic Items

I need...	...が要るんですが。	*...ga irun desu ga*
an adapter	アダプタ	*adaputa*
aluminum [kitchen] foil	アルミホイル	*arumi hoiru*
a bottle opener	栓抜き	*sen nuki*
a broom	箒	*hooki*
a can opener	缶切り	*kankiri*
cleaning supplies	クリーニング用品	*kuriiningu yoohin*
a corkscrew	コルクスクリュー	*koruku sukuryuu*
detergent	洗剤	*senzai*
dishwashing liquid	中性洗剤	*tyuusee senzai*
garbage [rubbish]	ごみ袋	*gomi bukuro*

bags		
a light bulb	電球	*denkyuu*
matches	マッチ	*matchi*
a mop	モップ	*moppu*
napkins	ナプキン	*napukin*
paper towels	ペーパータオル	*peepaa taoru*
plastic wrap [cling film]	ラップ	*rappu*
a plunger	トイレの吸引具	*toire no kyuuingu*
scissors	はさみ	*hasami*
a vacuum cleaner	掃除機	*soojiki*

For In the Kitchen, see page 76.

At the Hostel

Do you have any places left for tonight?	今晩、空いている部屋はありますか。	*konban aiteiru heya wa arimasuka*
Can I have…?	…をお願いします 。	*…o onegai shimasu*
a single/ double room	一人/二人 部屋	*hitori/futari beya*
a blanket	毛布	*moofu*
a pillow	枕	*makura*
sheets	シーツ	*shiitsu*
a towel	タオル	*taoru*
Do you have lockers?	ロッカーはありますか。	*rokkaa wa arimasu ka*
What time do you lock up?	正面玄関は、何時に閉まりますか。	*shoomen genkan wa nanji ni shimarimasu ka*
Do I need a membership card?	メンバーシップカードは必要です か。	*menbaa shippu kaado wa hitsuyoo desu ka*
Here's my international student card.	こちらが国際学生証です。	*kochira ga kokusai gakusei shoo desu*

There are over 500 youth hostels, or ユースホステル **yuusu hosuteru**, located in every part of Japan. They offer the most inexpensive accommodations available. You will often need to share rooms or bathrooms.

Going Camping

Can I camp here?	ここでキャンプできますか。
	koko de kyanpu dekimasu ka
Is there a campsite near here?	この近くに、キャンプ場はありますか。
	kono chikaku ni kyanpujoo wa arimasu ka
What is the charge per day/week?	一日/一週間の料金はいくらですか。
	ichi-nichi/isshuukan no ryookin wa ikura desu ka
Are there...?	...はありますか。 ...*wa arimasu ka*
cooking facilities	炊事場 *suijiba*
electrical outlets	電源 *dengen*
laundry facilities	洗濯場 *sentakuba*
showers	シャワー *shawaa*
tents for hire	貸しテント *kashi tento*
Where can I empty the chemical toilet?	ケミカルトイレの汚物を処理したいんですが。
	kemikaru toire no obutsu o shori shitain desu ga

YOU MAY SEE...

飲料水	drinking water
キャンプ禁止	no camping
焚火/バーベキュー禁止	no fires/barbecues

For Domestic Items, see page 45.
For In the Kitchen, see page 76.

Communications

ESSENTIAL

Where's an internet café?	インターネットカフェはどこですか。 *intaanetto kafe wa doko desu ka*
Can I access the internet/check e-mail?	インターネット/E メール を使いたいんです が。 *intaanetto/iimeeru o tsukaitain desu ga*
How much per (half) hour?	一(半)時間いくらですか。 *ichi(han)jikan ikura desu ka*
How do I connect / log on?	接続/ログオン したいんですが。 *setsuzoku/roguon shitain desu ga*
I'd like a phone card, please.	テレホンカードをください。 *terehon kaado o kudasai*
Can I have your phone number?	電話番号を教えてください。 *denwa bangoo o oshiete kudasai*
Here's my number/ e-mail address.	これが私の電話番号/E メールアドレス です。 *kore ga watashi no denwabangoo/iimeeru adoresu desu*
Call me.	電話してください。 *denwa shite kudasai*
E-mail me.	メールをください。 *meeru o kudasai*
Hello. This is...	もしもし。...ですが。 *moshi moshi...desu ga*
I'd like to speak to...	...さん、お願いします。 *...san onegai shimasu*
Could you repeat that, please?	もう一度、言ってください。 *moo ichido itte kudasai*
I'll call back later.	あとで電話します。 *ato de denwa shimasu*
Bye.	ごめんください。 *gomen kudasai*
Where's the post office?	郵便局はどこですか。 *yuubinkyoku wa doko desu ka*
I'd like to send this to...	これを ...に送りたいんですが。 *kore o...ni okuri tain desu ga*

Online

Where's an internet cafe?	インターネットカフェはどこですか。
	intaanetto kafe wa doko desu ka
Does it have wireless internet?	ワイアレスインターネットがありますか。
	waiaresu intaanetto ga arimasu ka
How do I turn the computer on/off?	コンピュータを点け/消したいんですが。
	konpyuuta o tsuke/keshi tain desu ga
What is the WiFi password?	無線LANのパスワードは何ですか。
	musen LAN no pasuwaado wa nandesuka
Is the WiFi free?	無線LAN は無料ですか 。
	musen LAN wa muryoo desuka
Can I access Skype?	スカイプにアクセスできますか
	sukaipu ni akusesu deki masu ka
Do you have bluetooth?	Bluetooth はありますか
	bluu twuusu wa ari masu ka
Can I...?	…いいですか。*...iidesuka*
plug in/charge my laptop/iPhone/iPad?	ラップトップ/iPhone/iPad の電源を つないでも/を充電しても
	rapputoppu / ai fon / ai paddo no dengen o tsunaidemo / o juuden shitemo
Can I...?	…ができますか。*...ga dekimasu ka*
access the internet	インターネットアクセス *intaanetto akusesu*
check e-mail	E メールのチェック *iimeeru no chekku*
print	印刷 *insatsu*
How much per (half) hour?	一(半)時間いくらですか。
	ichi(han)jikan ikura desu ka
How do I...?	…はどうしますか。*...wa doo shimasu ka*
connect	接続する *setsuzoku suru*
disconnect	接続を切る の *setsuzoku o kiru no*
log on/off	ログオン/ログオフ するの
	roguon/roguofu suru no

type this symbol	この記号をタイプするの *kono kigoo o taipu suru no*
What's your e-mail?	Eメールのアドレスは何ですか。
	iimeeru no adoresuwa nan desu ka
My e-mail is…	私のEメールアドレスは…
	watashi no iimeeru adoresu wa…
Do you have a scanner?	スキャナーはありますか。 *sukyanaa wa arimasu ka*

Social Media

Are you on Facebook /Twitter?	Facebook/Twitter に参加していますか。
	feisu bukku / tsuittaa ni sanka shite imasu ka
What's your user name?	ユーザーネームは何ですか。
	yuuzaa neemu wa nan desu ka
I'll add you as a friend.	友達に追加します。 *tomodachi ni tsuika shimasu*
I'll follow you on Twitter.	Twitter でフォローします。
	tsuittaa de foroo shimasu
Are you following…?	…をフォローしていますか。
	…o foroo shite imasu ka
I'll put the pictures on Facebook/Twitter.	Facebook/Twitter に写真を載せます。
	feisu bukku / tsuittaa ni shashin o nose masu
I'll tag you in the pictures.	あなたの写真にタグをつけます。
	anatano shashin ni tagu o tsuke masu

YOU MAY SEE...

閉じる	close
削除する	delete
Eメール	e-mail
ログアウト	exit
ヘルプ	help
インスタント・メッセージ	instant messenger
インターネット	internet
ログイン	login
新着メール	new (message)
オン/オフ	on/off
開ける	open
印刷する	print
保存	save
送信	send
ユーザー名/パスワード	username/password
無線インターネット/ ワイヤレスインターネット	wireless internet

Phone

A phonecard/prepaid phone, please.	テレホンカード/ プリペイド携帯 をお願いします。 *terehonkaado/puripeidokeitai o onegai shimasu*
How much?	いくらですか。*ikura desuka*
What's the area/ country code for...?	...の 市外局番/国番号 は何番ですか。 *...no shigaikyokuban/kunibangoo wa nanban desu ka*
What's the number for Information?	番号案内は何番ですか。 *bangoo an-nai wa nanban desu ka*
I'd like the number for...	...の番号を教えてください。 *...no bangooo oshiete kudasai*

Where's the pay phone?	公衆電話はどこですか。
	koosyuu denwa wa doko desu ka
My phone doesn't work here.	私の電話が使えません。
	watashi no denwa ga tsukaemasen
What network are you on?	どの電話会社をご使用ですか。
	dono denwa gaisha o goshiyoo desu ka
Is it 3G?	3Gですか。 *3G desu ka*
I have run out of credit/minutes.	クレジット/分数を使い果たしてしまいました。
	kurejitto / funsuu o tsukai hatashite shimai mashita
Can I buy some credit?	クレジットを買いたいのですが。
	kurejitto o kaitai no desu ga

YOU MAY HEAR...

どなたですか。 *donata desu ka*	Who's calling?
少々お待ちください。	Hold on.
shoo shoo omachi kudasai	
おつなぎします。 *otsunagi shimasu*	I'll put you through.
すみません。今、出ています。	I'm afraid he's/ she's
sumimasen ima dete imasu	not in.
ただ今、電話に出られません。	He/She can't come
tada ima denwa ni deraremasen	to the phone.
ご伝言を承りましょうか。	Would you like to leave a
godengon o uketamawarimashoo ka	message?
後程/十分後に お電話ください。	Call back later/in 10
nochihodo/juppungoni odenwa kudasai	minutes.
こちらからお電話いたしましょうか。	Can he/she call you back?
kochira kara odenwa itashimashoo ka	
お電話番号を頂けますか。	What's your number?
odenwa bangoo o itadakemasu ka	

You can find public phones in hotel lobbies, on the street and in train stations. You will be able to make overseas phone calls using coins, prepaid telephone cards purchased at a convenience store, or your credit card.

Country codes: Canada and US are +1, UK is +44. Directory assistance in English: 0120-364-463 110 (police) or 119 (fire).

A prepaid phone, please.	プリペイドフォンをお願いします。 *puripeido fon o onegai shimasu*
Do you have a phone charger?	携帯用の充電器はありますか 。 *keitaiyoo no juudenki wa arimasu ka*
Can I have your number?	電話番号を教えてください。 *denwa bangoo o oshiete kudasai*
Here's my number.	これが私の電話番号です。 *korega watashi no denwa bangoo desu*
Call me.	電話してください。 *denwa shite kudasai*
Text me.	携帯にメールを送ってください。 *keitai ni meeru o okutte kudasai*
I'll call you.	電話します。 *denwa shimasu*
I'll text you.	メールを送ります。 *meeru o okurimasu*

Telephone Etiquette

Hello. This is...	もしもし。...ですが。 *moshi moshi...desu ga*
I'd like to speak to...	...さん、お願いします。 *...san onegai shimasu*
Extension...	内線...番 *naisen...ban*
Speak louder/more slowly, please.	もう少し 大きい声で/ゆっくり お願いします。 *mooo sukoshi ookii koe de/yukkuri onegai shimasu*
Could you repeat that, please?	もう一度、言ってください。 *moo ichido itte kudasai*
I'll call back later.	あとで電話します。 *atode denwa shimasu*
Bye.	ごめんください。 *gomen kudasai*

Fax

Can I send/receive a fax here?	ここでファックスを 送れ/受け取れますか。 *kokode fakkusu o okure/uketore masu ka*
What's the fax number?	ファックスの番号を頂けますか。 *fakkusu no bangoo o itadakemasu ka*
Please fax this to...	これを ...にファックスしてください。 *kore o...ni fakkusu shite kudasai*

Main post offices are open from 8:00 a.m. to 7:00 p.m. on weekdays, 9:00 a.m. to 5:00 p.m. on Saturdays and 9:00 a.m. to 12:30 p.m. on Sundays. Local post offices do not open on Sundays and will have limited hours mid-week. Tokyo International Post Office is open around the clock. Stamps are also sold at hotels and some tobacconists. Mailboxes, usually red, are found on street corners. You can also mail letters at hotels.

YOU MAY HEAR...

税関申告書に記入してください。
zeikan shinkokusho ni kinyuu shite kudasai

どのくらいの値段のものですか。
dono kurai no nedan no mono desu ka

中には何が入っていますか。
naka niwa nani ga haitte imasu ka

Please fill out the customs declaration form.
What's the value?

What's inside?

Post

Where's the post office/mailbox [postbox]?	郵便局/郵便ポスト はどこですか。 *yuubinkyoku/yuubin posuto wa doko desu ka*
A stamp for this postcard/letter, please.	この葉書/手紙用の切手をください。 *kono hagaki/tegami yoo no kitte o kudasai*
How much?	いくらですか 。*ikura desuka*
I want to send this package by airmail/express	この小包を速達/航空便で送りたいんですが。 *kono kozutsumi o sokutatsu/kookuubin de okuritain desu ga*
A receipt, please.	レシートをお願いします。*reshiito o onegai shimasu*

Food & Drink

ESSENTIAL

Can you recommend a good restaurant/ bar?	いいレストラン/バー をご存知ですか。 *ii resutoran/baa o gozonji desu ka*
Is there a traditional Japanese/inexpensive restaurant nearby?	この近くに料亭/安いレストラン はあります か。 *kono chikaku ni ryootei/yasui resutoran wa arimasu ka*
A table for one/two, please.	一人/二人ですが、テーブルがありますか。 *hitori/futari desu ga, teeburu ga arimasu ka*
Could we sit…?	…に座れますか。*…ni suwaremasu ka*
here/there	ここ/そこ *koko/soko*
outside	外 *soto*
in a non-smoking area	禁煙席 *kin en seki*
I'm waiting for someone.	人を待っているんです。*hito o matte irun desu*
Where's the restroom [toilet]?	トイレはどこですか。*toire wa doko desu ka*
A menu, please.	メニューをお願いします。 *menyuu o onegai shimasu*
What do you recommend?	何がおいしいですか。*nani ga oishii desu ka*
I'd like…	…が欲しいんですが …*ga hoshiin desu ga*
Some more…, please.	…をお願いします。*…o onegai shimasu*
Enjoy your meal.	どうぞごゆっくり。*doozo goyukkuri*
The check [bill], please.	お勘定、お願いします。*okanjoo onegai shimasu*

57

Is service included?	サービス料込みですか。
	saabisuryoo komi desu ka
Can I pay by credit card?	クレジットカードを使えますか。
	kurejitto kaado o tsukaemasu ka
Could I have a receipt, please?	レシートをお願いします。
	reshiito o onegai shimasu
Thank you for the food.	ごちそうさまでした。 *gochisoo sama deshita*

Where to Eat

Can you recommend...?	...はありますか。... *wa arimasu ka*
a restaurant	レストラン *resutoran*
a bar	バー *baa*
a cafe	カフェ *kafe*
a fast-food place	ファストフードの店 *fasuto fuudo no mise*
a sushi restaurant	寿司屋 *sushi ya*
a cheap restaurant	安いレストラン *yasui resutoran*
an expensive restaurant	高いレストラン *takai resutoran*
a restaurant with a good view	眺めの良いレストラン *nagame no yoi resutoran*
an authentic/ a non-touristy restaurant	庶民的な/観光客向けでないレストラン
	syominteki na / kankookyaku muke de nai resutoran

Reservations & Preferences

I'd like to reserve a table...	...予約をお願いしたいんですが。
	yoyaku o onegai shitai n desu ga
for 2	2人で *futari de*
for this evening	今晩 *konban*
for tomorrow at...	明日...時に *ashita...ji ni*

Can I get a table in the shade/sun?	日陰の/日向のテーブルをお願いします。 *hikage no / hinata no teeburu o onegai shimasu*
A table for 2.	2 人、お願いします。 *futari onegai shimasu*
We have a reservation.	予約してあります。 *yoyaku shite arimasu*
My name is...	...です。 *...desu*
Could we sit...?	...に座れますか。 *...ni suwaremasu ka*
here/there	ここ/そこ *koko/soko*
outside	外 *soto*
in a non-smoking area	禁煙席 *kin enseki*
by the window	窓際 *madogiwa*
in the shade	日陰に *hikage ni*
in the sun	日向に *hinata ni*
Where are the restrooms [toilets]?	トイレはどこですか。 *toire wa doko desu ka*

YOU MAY HEAR...

ご予約はいただいておりますでしょうか。 *goyoyaku wa itadaite orimasu deshoo ka*	Do you have a reservation?
何人様でしょうか。 *nannin sama deshoo ka*	How many?
喫煙席と禁煙席のどちらがよろしいですか。 *kitsuenseki to kin-enseki no dochira ga yoroshii desu ka*	Smoking or non-smoking?
ご注文はお決まりですか。 *gochuumon wa okimari desu ka*	Are you ready to order?
何がよろしいですか。 *nani ga yoroshii desu ka*	What would you like?
...がお薦めです。 *...ga osusume desu*	I recommend...
どうぞごゆっくり。 *doozo goyukkuri*	Enjoy your meal.

How to Order

Waiter!/Waitress!	ちょっとすみません。*chotto sumimasen*
We're ready to order.	注文したいんですが。*chuumon shitain desu ga*
May I see the wine list, please?	ワインリストをお願いします。*wain risuto o onegai shimasu*
I'd like...	...が欲しいんですが ...*ga hoshiin desu ga*
a bottle of...	...を一本 ...*o ippon*
a carafe of...	...を一カラフ ...*o hito karafu*
a glass of...	...一杯 ...*ippai*
The menu, please.	メニューをお願いします。*menyuu o onegaishimasu*
Do you have...?	...は、ありますか。*...wa arimasu ka*
a menu in English	英語のメニュー *eigo no menyuu*
a fixed price menu	セットメニュー *setto menyuu*
a children's menu	子供用のメニュー *kodomo yoo no menyuu*
What do you recommend?	何がおいしいですか。*nani ga oishii desu ka*
What's this?	これは何ですか。*kore wan nan desu ka*
What's in it?	何が入っていますか。*nani ga haitte imasu ka*
Is it spicy?	これは辛いですか。*kore wa karai desu ka*
Some more ..., please	...を、もう少しお願いします。*...o moo sukoshi onegai shimasu*
It's to go [take away].	持ち帰りです。*mochi kaeri desu*
With/Without...	...と/...無しで *...to/...nashi de*

YOU MAY SEE...

カバーチャージ	cover charge
セット値段	fixed-price
メニュー	menu
本日のメニュー	menu of the day
サービス料金込(別)	service (not) included
スペシャル	specials

I can't have…	…は食べられません。	…wa taberaremasen
I'd like…	…が欲しいんですが。	…ga hoshiin desu ga
More… please	…をもっとください。	…o motto kudasai

For Drinks, see page 77.

Cooking Methods

baked	焼き	yaki
boiled	茹で	yude
braised	蒸し煮	mushini
breaded	パン粉	panko
creamed	クリームソース	kuriimu soosu
diced	さいの目切りの	sai no me giri no
filleted	切り身の	kiri mi no
fried	揚げ	age
grilled	焼き	yaki
poached	ポシェ	poshe
roasted	ロースト	roosuto
sautéed	炒めた	itameta
smoked	薫製	kunsei
steamed	蒸し	mushi
stewed	煮込み	nikomi
stuffed	詰め物	tsumemono

Dietary Requirements

I am…	私は…です。	watashi wa… desu
diabetic	糖尿病	toonyoobyoo
lactose intolerant	乳糖不対症	nyuutoo futaishoo
vegetarian	ベジタリアン	bejitarian
vegan	ヴィーガン	biigan
I'm allergic to…	…にアレルギーがあります。	…ni arerugii ga arimasu
I can't eat…	…は食べられません。	…wa taberaremasen
dairy	乳製品	nyuuseehin

gluten	グルテン *guruten*
nuts	ナッツ *nattsu*
pork	豚肉 *buta niku*
shellfish	貝類 *kairui*
spicy foods	辛い食べ物 *karai tabemono*
wheat	小麦 *komugi*
Is it halal/kosher?	これは ハラール/コーシャ ですか。 *kore wa haraaru/koosha desu ka*
Do you have…?	…はありますか。*…wa arimasu ka*
skimmed milk	無脂肪乳 *mushiboo nyuu*
whole milk	普通の牛乳 *futsuu no gyuunyuu*
soya milk	豆乳 *toonyuu*
I'm lactose intolerant…	私は乳製品アレルギーがあります。 *watashi ha nyuseihin arerugi ga arimasu.*

Dining with Children

Do you have children's portions?	お子さまメニューはありますか。 *okosama menyuu wa arimasu ka*
A highchair, please.	子供のための椅子はありますか。 *kodomo no tame no isu wa arimasu ka*
Where can I feed/ change the baby?	どこで 授乳したら/ おしめを取り替えたら いいでしょうか。 *doko de junyuu shitara/oshime o torikaetara ii deshoo ka*
Can you warm this?	これを暖めてください。*kore o atatamete kudaasai*

How to Complain

How much longer will our food be?	後、どのくらいかかりますか。 *ato dono kurai kakarimasu ka*
We can't wait any longer.	もう待てません。*moo matemasen*
We're leaving.	帰ります。*kaerimasu*

I didn't order this.	注文したのと違います。
	chuumon shitano to chigaimasu
I ordered...	...を注文しました。*...o chuumon shimashita*
I can't eat this.	これは、食べられません。*kore wa taberaremasen*
This is too...	...すぎます 。*...sugimasu*
cold/hot	冷た/熱 *tsumeta/atsu*
salty/spicy	塩辛/辛 *shio kara/kara*
tough/bland	固/味が薄 *kata/aji ga usu*
This isn't clean/fresh.	きれい/新鮮 じゃありません。
	kiree/shinsen ja arimasen

Paying

The check [bill], please.	お勘定、お願いします。*okanjoo onegai shimasu*
We'd like to pay separately.	別々に、お願いします。*betsubetsu ni onegai shimasu*
It's all together.	一緒にお願いします。*issho ni onegai shimasu*
Is service included?	サービス料込みですか。*saabisu ryoo komi desu ka*
What's this amount for?	これは何の金額ですか。*kore wa nan no kingaku desu ka*
I didn't have that.	それは取りませんでした。*sore wa torimasen deshita.*
I had...	注文したのは...です。
	chuumon shita nowa...desu
Can I pay by credit card?	クレジットカードを使えますか。
	kurejitto kaado o tsukaemasu ka
Can I have an itemized bill/a receipt?	明細書/レシート をお願いします。
	meesaisho/reshiito o onegai shimasu

Tipping is not a Japanese custom, and there is no need to tip at most restaurants, bars and **izakaya** (taverns). However, some places, especially high-end ones, may include a 'service charge' on the bill as gratuity.

That was a very good meal.	おいしかった。ごちそうさまでした。
	oishikatta. gochisoo sama deshita.
I've already paid.	もう支払いは済ませました。
	moo shiharai wa sumase mashita

Meals & Cooking

In large Western-style hotels you will have your choice of breakfast: Japanese, English/American or Continental. However, in **ryokan** and **minshuku** (traditional Japanese lodgings) you will be offered only a Japanese-style breakfast. This usually consists of grilled, smoked fish (e.g. salmon), rice, soup and pickles served with tea. While you are out and about, coffee shops provide various dishes for breakfast, including thick slices of buttered toast.

Breakfast

bacon	ベーコン *beekon*
bread	パン *pan*
butter	バター *bataa*
(cold/hot) cereal	(コールド/ホット)シリアル
	(koorudo/hotto) shiriaru
cheese	チーズ *chiizu*
coffee/tea	コーヒー/紅茶 *koohii/koocha*
with sugar	砂糖入りの *satoo iri no*
with artificial	ダイエットシュガー 入りの
sweetner	*daietto shugaa iri no*
with milk	ミルク入りの *miruku iri no*

decaf	カフェイン抜きの *kafein nuki no*
black	ブラック *burakku*
cold cuts [charcuterie]	コールドカット *koorudo katto*
eggs	卵 *tamago*
a boiled egg	ゆで卵 *yude tamago*
fried/scrambled eggs	目玉焼き/スクランブルエッグ *medama yaki/sukuranburu eggu*
fruit juice	フルーツジュース *furuutsu juusu*
apple	アップル *appuru*
grapefruit	グレープフルーツ *gureepufuruutsu*
orange	オレンジ *orenji*
granola [muesli]	グラノーラ *guranoora*
honey	蜂蜜 *hachimitsu*
jam	ジャム *jamu*
milk	ミルク *miruku*
muffin	マフィン *mafin*
oatmeal	オートミール *ooto miiru*
omelet	オムレツ *omuretsu*
rolls	ロールパン *rooru pan*
sausages	ソーセージ *sooseeji*
toast	トースト *toosuto*
water	水 *mizu*
yogurt	ヨーグルト *yooguruto*

Appetizers

assorted appetizers	オードブルの盛り合わせ *oodoburu no moriawase*
ham	ハム *hamu*
I'd like...	...が欲しいんですが。 *...ga hoshiin desu ga*
More... please	...をもっとください。 *...o motto kudasai*
Japanese snacks	おつまみ *otsumami*
Japanese pickled	漬物 *tsukemono*

Otsumami are snacks that accompany drinks. You will find such things as salted rice crackers, nuts and dried cuttle fish.

vegetables		
olives	オリーブ	*oriibu*
oysters	牡蛎	*kaki*
salad	サラダ	*sarada*
salami	サラミ	*sarami*

Soup

clear soup	コンソメスープ	*konsome suupu*
creamed soup	ポタージュスープ	*potaaju suupu*
Japanese clear soup	すまし汁(お吸物)	*sumashi jiru (osuimono)*
miso soup	みそ汁	*misoshiru*
sweetcorn soup	コーンスープ	*koon suupu*
vegetable soup	野菜スープ	*yasai suupu*
thick soup of chicken, shellfish, prawns, bean curd and vegetables	寄せ鍋	*yosenabe*
Chinese noodle broth with meat, fish, veg	ラーメン	*raamen*
clear soup of fish bouillon or seaweed	吸物/すまし汁	*suimono/sumashi jiru*
wheat noodles in a thick bouillon with fish cake and vegetables	あんかけうどん	*ankake udon*
Chinese noodle soup with fried veg	タンメン	*tanmen*
thinly cut wheat	冷麦	*hiyamugi*

There are two kinds of Japanese soup, which is always part of a traditional meal: **misoshiru**, a light soup often with a few finely chopped pieces of vegetable and bean curd, the distinctive flavor of which comes from the fermented bean paste (**miso**); and **sumashi jiru** or **suimono**, a clear soup, again with vegetables or bean curd. In a Japanese meal the soup is not served as a first course, but together with the main course, or with boiled rice and other items.

noodles and cold soup		
buckwheat noodles served with cold soup	ざるそば	*zaru soba*
Chinese noodles sweet and sour sauce, sliced ham, fish cake and cucumber	冷やし中華	*hiyashi chuuka*
a winter soup with veg, fish cake, eggs	おでん	*oden*

Fish & Seafood

bonito (mackerel family)	鰹(カツオ)	*katsuo*
cod	鱈(タラ)	*tara*
cod roe	たらこ	*tarako*
lobster	ロブスター	*robusutaa*
mackerel	鯖(サバ)	*saba*
mussels	ムール貝	*muuru gai*
octopus	蛸(タコ)	*tako*
oysters	牡蠣(カキ)	*kaki*
salmon	鮭(サケ)	*sake*

salmon roe	いくら	*ikura*
scallop	帆立貝	*hotate gai*
squid	いか	*ika*
shrimp [prawns]	海老(エビ)	*ebi*
trout	鱒(マス)	*masu*
tuna	鮪(マグロ)	*maguro*
whitebait	白子(シラス)	*shirasu*
raw fish with soy and wasabi	刺身	*sashimi*
rice balls with raw fish	寿司	*sushi*
grilled fish	焼き魚	*yaki zakana*
fresh fish, seafood and	天ぷら	*tenpura*

Fish and seafood play a major role in Japanese cuisine. This is reflected in the variety and quality of available seafood. Typical ways of eating fish include broiled, boiled, deep fried and raw. Prepared raw fish (**sushi** or **sashimi**) is dipped into a mixture of soy sauce and **wasabi** (horseradish paste), and enjoyed with steaming hot rice. **Sashimi** is usually served as part of a larger meal, and **sashimi** restaurants are often expensive. You can also buy **sushi** at the food court of a department store, at a supermarket, or at a take-out restaurant.

veg, deep-fried

battered fish and veg in a noodle broth	天ぷらうどん *tenpura udon*
fish cooked in assorted sauces	煮魚 *ni zakana*
fish and veg broth	ちり鍋 *chirinabe*

Meat & Poultry

bacon	ベーコン *beekon*
beef	牛肉 *gyuu niku*
chicken	鶏肉/チキン *tori niku/chikin*
duck	鴨 *kamo*
filet steak	ひれステーキ *hire suteeki*
ham	ハム *hamu*
lamb	ラム肉 *ramu niku*
liver	レバー *rebaa*
pork	豚肉 *buta niku*
sausages	ソーセージ *sooseeji*
steak	ステーキ *suteeki*
sirloin steak	サーロインステーキ *saaroin suteeki*
thin slices	薄切り *usugiri*
thin slices of beef, veg, bean curd, noodles	すき焼 *sukiyaki*
thinly sliced beef with veg in broth	しゃぶしゃぶ *shabu shabu*
Grilled Korean marinated meat, veg	焼肉 *yaki niku*
fried breaded pork cutlet with cabbage and rice	とんかつ *tonkatsu*
deep fried pork with rice, egg, onion, peas	カツ丼 *katsudon*

barbequed chicken in sweet soy sauce	焼き鳥 *yakitori*
rare	レア *rea*
medium	ミディアム *midiamu*
well-done	ウェルダン *werudan*

Vegetables & Staples

boiled green vegetables with soy sauce	おひたし *ohitashi*
beans	豆 *mame*
bread	パン *pan*
buckwheat noodles	そば *soba*

In a Japanese meal, rice is served separately in an individual bowl. It is short grained and slightly sticky. Although plain, rice is perhaps the most important part of the meal. The Japanese consider it a heresy to mix other food items or sauces into the rice. It is customary to raise the bowl to your lips and push the rice into your mouth with chopsticks. On a Western-style menu rice is usually called **raisu**. For egg and rice dishes, go to the On the Menu section on page 84 and look under 'egg'.

Salad isn't part of traditional Japanese cuisine; pickled vegetables are a more authentic equivalent. However, many Western-style restaurants and bars offer a variety of salads and dressings.

cabbage	キャベツ	*kyabetsu*
carrot	にんじん	*ninjin*
Chinese cabbage	白菜	*hakusai*
Chinese noodles in soup	ラーメン	*raamen*
cucumber	きゅうり	*kyuuri*
eggplant [aubergine]	なす	*nasu*
gingko nut	ぎんなん	*ginnan*
green bean	さやいんげん	*saya ingen*
Japanese pickled vegetables	漬物	*tsukemono*
leek	ねぎ	*negi*
lettuce	レタス	*retasu*
pasta	パスタ	*pasuta*
MSG (monosodium glutamate)	味の素	*aji no moto*
mushroom	マッシュルーム	*masshuruumu*
shitake mushroom	椎茸(しいたけ)	*shiitake*
enokidake mushroom	えのきだけ	*enokidake*

Noodle dishes are very popular, and make delicious and filling meals. It's not considered bad manners to make slurping noises while eating your noodles — the extra oxygen is supposed to improve the taste. For dishes, see 'noodle' on page 87 in the On the Menu section.

onion	玉ねぎ *tamanegi*
pea	グリンピース *gurinpiisu*
potato (in Western dishes)	ポテト *poteto*
potato (in Japanese dishes)	じゃがいも *jagaimo*
pumpkin	かぼちゃ *kabocha*
rice	ご飯 *gohan*
spaghetti	スパゲッティ *supagetti*
stir-fried vegetables	野菜炒め *yasai itame*
stewed vegetables	野菜の煮物 *yasai no nimono*
tomato	トマト *tomato*
white radish	大根 *daikon*
wheat noodles	うどん *udon*

Fruit

apple	りんご *ringo*
banana	バナナ *banana*
cherry	さくらんぼ *sakuranbo*
grapefruit	グレープフルーツ *gureepufuruutsu*
grape	ぶどう *budoo*
melon	メロン *meron*
orange	オレンジ *orenji*
peach	桃 *momo*
pear	梨 *nashi*
persimmon	柿 *kaki*
strawberry	苺(いちご) *ichigo*
tangerine	蜜柑(みかん) *mikan*
watermelon	西瓜(すいか) *suika*

Dessert is not a typical part of a Japanese meal. Called **dezaato**, it was introduced from the West. Today you will find a variety of Western-style desserts along with a number of desserts made from more typical Japanese ingredients.

Dessert

rice cake, traditionally eaten at New Year	餅	*mochi*
gelatin cubes made from seaweed, with sweet bean paste and fruit	あんみつ	*anmitsu*
sweet bean paste covered with shaved ice and sweet syrup	氷あずき	*koori azuki*
gelatin cubes made from seaweed, topped with fruit and syrup	フルーツみつ豆	*furuutsu mitsumame*
crème caramel	プリン	*purin*
ice cream	アイスクリーム	*aisu kuriimu*
hot steamed bun with sweet azuki bean paste	あんまん	*anman*
chocolate parfait	チョコレートパフェ	*chokoreeto pafe*
arrowroot cake with molasses syrup	葛餅	*kuzu moch*
sweet pancake with butter and syrup	ホットケーキ	*hotto keeki*
fruit salad	フルーツサラダ	*furuutsu sarada*

In Japan, goods are usually sold in small portions to avoid selling them in certain numbers as some numbers are considered bad luck. Vegetables are usually sold per piece, or in pre-packaged bags that are quite uniform in volume. The weight is not marked (e.g. a bag of potatoes contains five potatoes). Prices for fish vary according to type and season and are sold per unit, not by the kilogram.

balls of rice covered with bean paste	おはぎ	*ohagi*
sweet red bean paste soup	お汁粉	*oshiruko*

Sauces & Condiments

black pepper	コショウ/胡椒	*koshoo*
ketchup	ケチャップ	*kechappu*
miso (paste of fermented soybeans)	味噌	*miso*
mustard	マスタード	*masutaado*
salt	塩	*shio*
soy sauce	醤油	*shooyu*

YOU MAY HEAR...

いらっしゃいませ。*irasshaimase*	Can I help you?
何がよろしいですか。*naniga yoroshii desu ka*	What would you like?
他に何かございますか。 *hokani nanika gozaimasu ka*	Anything else?
…円でございます。*…en de gozaimasu*	That's…yen.

For daily shopping, people usually go to a neighborhood fish market, vegetable store, butcher or grocer. Larger supermarkets are also popular, as well as food floors of department stores (usually located in the basement) where you'll find groceries and prepared food. In Tokyo there is a famous fish market called **Tsukiji Uoichiba**, which is open early in the morning. In Kyoto, **Nishiki Shijo** (Nishiki Market) is called the kitchen of Kyoto. Here you can find all kinds of local ingredients at more than one hundred stores.

YOU MAY SEE...

賞味期限...	best if used by...
カロリー	calories
無脂肪	fat free
要冷蔵	keep refrigerated
...を極少量含む	may contain traces of...
販売期限	sell by...
菜食主義者向け	suitable for vegetarians

At the Market

Where are the carts [trolleys]/baskets?	カート/かごはどこですか。 *kaato/kago wa doko desu ka*
Where is...?	...はどこですか。 *...wa doko desu ka*
I'd like some of that/those.	それを少しください。 *sore o sukoshi kudasai*
Can I taste it?	味見してもいいですか。 *ajimi shitemo ii desu ka*
I'd like a kilo/half-kilo of...	...が一キロ/五百グラム欲しいんですが *...ga ichikiro/gohyakuguramu hoshiin desu ga*

I'd like...	...が欲しいんですが *...ga hoshiin desu ga*
a liter/half-liter of...	...が一リットル/500cc *... ga iti rittoru/gohyaku shiishii*
a piece of	...が一個 *...ga ikko*
a slice of	...が一枚 *...ga ichimai*
More/Less than that	もう少し 多く/少なく *moo sukoshi ooku/sukunaku*
How much?	いくらですか。 *ikura desuka*
Where do I pay?	どこで払うんですか。 *doko de haraun desu ka*
A bag, please.	袋をお願いします。 *fukuro o onegai shimasu*
I'm being helped.	大丈夫です。 *daijoobu desu*

In the Kitchen

bottle opener	栓抜き *sennuki*
bowl	ボール *booru*
can opener	缶切り *kankiri*
corkscrew	コルクスクリュー *koruku sukuryuu*
cups	カップ *kappu*
forks	フォーク *fooku*
frying pan	フライパン *furaipan*
glasses	グラス/コップ *gurasu/koppu*
knife	ナイフ *naifu*
measuring cup/spoon	計量カップ/スプーン *keeryoo kappu/supuun*
napkin	ナプキン *napukin*
plates	皿 *sara*
pot	深鍋 *fuka nabe*
saucepan	鍋 *nabe*
spatula	へら *hera*
spoon	スプーン *supuun*

Drinks

ESSENTIAL

May I see the wine list/drink menu?	ワインリスト/ドリンクメニュー を見せてください。 *wain risuto/dorinku menyuu o misete kudasai*
What do you recommend?	何がおいしいですか。*nani ga oishii desu ka*
I'd like a bottle/glass of red/white wine.	赤/白 ワインを一本/一杯お願いします。 *aka/shiro wain o ippon/ippai onegai shimasu*
The house wine, please.	ハウスワインをお願いします。 *hausu wain o onegai shimasu*
Another bottle/glass, please.	もう一本/一杯お願いします。 *moo ippon/ippai onegai shimasu*
I'd like a local beer.	地ビールをお願いします。*jibiiru o onegai shimasu*
Can I buy you a drink?	一杯おごらせてください。*ippai ogorasete kudasai*
Cheers!	乾杯! *kanpai*
A coffee/tea, please.	コーヒー/紅茶をお願いします。 *koohii/koocha o onegai shimasu*
Black	ブラック *burakku*
With...	...と...*to*
milk	ミルク *miruku*
sugar	砂糖 *satoo*
artificial sweetener	ダイエットシュガー *daietto shugaa*
With/Without...	...と/...無しで ...*to/...nashi de*
I can't have...	...は食べられません ...*wa taberaremasen*
I'd like...	...をお願いします。...*o onegai shimasu*
juice	フルーツジュース *furuutsu juusu*
soda	炭酸飲料 *tansan inryoo*
sparkling/still water	ソーダ水/水 *soda sui/mizu*
Is the tap water safe to drink?	水道水は飲んでも安全ですか。 *suidoosui wa nondemo anzen desu ka*

Non-alcoholic Drinks

coffee	コーヒー	*koohii*
black	ブラック	*burakku*
with milk	ミルク入りの	*miruku irino*
with sugar	砂糖 入りの	*satoo iri no*
with artificial sweetner	ダイエットシュガー入りの	*daietto shugaa iri no*
iced coffee	アイスコーヒー	*aisu koohii*
hot chocolate	ココア	*kokoa*
juice	ジュース	*juusu*
apple juice	アップルジュース	*appuru juusu*
orange juice	オレンジジュース	*orenji juusu*
lemonade	レモネード	*remoneedo*
milk (when ordering at a restaurant)	ミルク	*miruku*
milkshake	ミルクセーキ	*mirukuseeki*

Sake is the general name for any drink, traditional or imported, but is usually used to refer to rice wine, more properly k nown as **nihonshu**.

Japanese green tea is often served in restaurants free of charge. It is drunk without any additions.

A special tea, **matcha** is used for traditional ceremonies. It was first used by Buddhist monks to help them stay awake while meditating. Its spiritual roots are still apparent today in the highly ritualized tea ceremony. The tea should not only refresh you physically, but also give you time to appreciate the beauty of the objects used in the ceremony and the surroundings, all leading to meditative reflection. You may find tea-ceremony rooms in museums and gardens, where you'll be able to try a little **matcha** for a small fee.

YOU MAY HEAR...

何か飲みますか。*nani ka nomimasu ka*
ミルク/砂糖 を入れますか。
miruku/satoo o iremasu ka

Can I get you a drink?
With milk/sugar?

炭酸水ですか,非炭酸水ですか。
tansansui desu ka hi tansansui desu ka

Sparkling or
still water?

tea	紅茶 *koocha*
green tea	お茶 *ocha*
iced tea	アイスティー *aisu tii*
water	水 *mizu*
mineral water	ミネラルウォーター *mineraru wootaa*
soda water	ソーダ *sooda*
tonic water	トニック *tonikku*

Aperitifs, Cocktails & Liqueurs

single/double	シングル/ダブル *shinguru/daburu*
straight [neat]/ on the rocks	ストレート/オンザロック *sutoreeto/onzarokku*
a glass/a bottle	グラス1杯/瓶1本 *gurasu ippai/bin ippon*
brandy	ブランデー *burandee*
gin	ジン *jin*
gin and tonic	ジントニック *jin tonikku*
plum wine	梅酒 *umeshu*
rum	ラム酒 *ramu shu*
sherry/vermouth	シェリー/ベルモット *sherii/berumotto*
shoochuu	焼酎 *shoochuu*
vodka	ウォッカ *wokka*
whisky	ウイスキー *uisukii*

| with water | 水割り *mizuwari* |
| with soda water | ウイスキーソーダ *uisukii sooda* |

Beer

bottled	瓶入り *bin iri*
draft [draught]	生 *nama*
dark beer	黒ビール *kuro biiru*

The Japanese produce a number of different beers which are similar to English and German lager beers. Three well known-brands are Asahi®, Kirin® and Sapporo®. In most bars you can choose between bottled and draft.

Shoochuu is a distilled liquor (up to 90 proof) made from either sweet potatoes or rice. This drink is not commonly known to visitors to Japan and is held in rather low esteem by some Japanese. The best **shoochuu** is, however, excellent and is comparable to tequila, vodka, and other such spirits. Whisky is now a very popular drink in Japan and there are a number of good Japanese brands — the best known is probably Suntory®.

Grape wine isn't an authentic Japanese drink and until recently was not produced in Japan. You will not find wine widely available outside of Western-style restaurants, big hotels, and department stores. Even there you may find the choice limited to sweeter white wines, although this is changing.

Rice wine, known as **nihonshu** but usually referred to as **sake**, is the traditional Japanese wine. The snacks traditionally served with sake are known as **otsumami**. These include seafood and meat served on skewers, sweet-salty dried cuttlefish, sashimi and more.

This drink is served at table in small china carafes and is drunk from small cups or wooden boxes. You can ask for your **nihonshu** to be served cold, warm or hot.

Wine

red wine	赤ワイン *aka wain*
white wine	白ワイン *shiro wain*
blush [rosé] wine	ロゼ *roze*
dry/sweet/sparkling	ドライ/スイート/スパークリング *dorai/suiito/supaakuringu*
chilled/at room temperature	冷えた/室温の *hieta/shitsuon no*
sake/nihonshu	お酒/日本酒 *osake/nihonshu*
cold	冷 *hiya*
lukewarm	人肌 *hitohada*
hot	熱燗 *atsukan*

On the Menu

almond	アーモンド *aamondo*
aperitif	食前酒 *shokuzenshu*
apple	りんご *ringo*
apple juice	アップルジュース *appuru juusu*
apricot	アンズ *anzu*
artichoke	アーティチョーク *aatichooku*
artificial sweetner	ダイエットシュガー *daietto shugaa*
asparagus	アスパラバス *asuparagasu*
avocado	アボカド *abokado*
bacon	ベーコン *beekon*
banana	バナナ *banana*
bass	バス *basu*
bay leaf	ベイリーフ *bei riifu*
bean	豆 *mame*
bean sprout	もやし *moyashi*
beef	牛肉 *gyuu niku*
beer	ビール *biiru*
beet	ビート *biito*
black pepper	胡椒 *koshoo*

blush [rosé] wine	ロゼ	*roze*
bonito (mackerel family)	鰹(カツオ)	*katsuo*
brandy	ブランデー	*burandee*
bread	パン	*pan*
breast chicken	胸肉	*muneniku*
broth	コンソメ	*konsome*
buckwheat noodles	そば	*soba*
butter	バター	*bataa*
cabbage	キャベツ	*kyabetsu*
carrot	にんじん	*ninjin*
cauliflower	カリフラワー	*karifurawaa*
celery	セロリ	*serori*
cheese	チーズ	*chiizu*
cherry	さくらんぼ	*sakuranbo*
chicken	鶏肉	*tori niku*
chickpea	ひよこ豆	*hiyoko mame*
Chinese cabbage	白菜	*hakusai*
Chinese meat dumplings	餃子	*gyooza*
Chinese noodle soup	ラーメン	*raamen*
chocolate	チョコレート	*chokoreeto*
cod	鱈(タラ)	*tara*
cod roe	たらこ	*tarako*
coffee	コーヒー	*koohii*
cookie [biscuit]	クッキー	*kukkii*
cornmeal	コーンミール	*koon miiru*
crab	蟹	*kani*
cracker	クラッカー	*kurakkaa*
cream	生クリーム	*namakuriimu*
cucumber	きゅうり	*kyuuri*

curried	カレー *karee*
custard	カスタード *kasutaado*
deep-fried	揚げ *age*
dried squid	するめ *surume*
duck	鴨 *kamo*
dumpling	餃子 *gyooza*
eel	鰻 *unagi*
egg	卵 *tamago*
thick sweet omelet	卵焼き *tamago yaki*
fried eggs	目玉焼き *medama yaki*
omelet	オムレツ *omuretsu*
omelet with fried rice and ketchup	オムライス *omuraisu*
egg custard with veg, fish and chicken	茶碗蒸し *chawan mushi*
set menu: rice, soup, fish or meat, pickles	定食 *teeshoku*
fried rice with pork, egg, peas and shrimp	炒飯 *chaahan*
Japanese curry	カレーライス *karee raisu*
eggplant [aubergine]	なす *nasu*
endive	エンダイブ *endaibu*
escarole	キクヂシャ *kikujisha*
fig	いちじく *ichijiku*
fish	魚 *sakana*
fish cake	蒲鉾 *kamaboko*
French fries [chips]	ポテトフライ *poteto furai*
fruit	フルーツ/果物 *furuutsu/kudamono*
fruit salad	フルーツサラダ *furuutsu sarada*
garlic	ニンニク *ninniku*
gin	ジン *jin*

ginger	生姜	*shooga*
gingko nuts	ぎんなん	*ginnan*
granola [muesli]	グラノーラ	*guranoora*
grapefruit	グレープフルーツ	*gureepufuruutsu*
grape	ぶどう/葡萄	*budoo*
green bean	さやいんげん	*saya ingen*
green tea	お茶	*ocha*
grilled tofu	焼き豆腐	*yaki doofu*
guava	グアバ	*guaba*
ham	ハム	*hamu*
hamburger	ハンバーガー	*hanbaagaa*
hazlenut	ヘーゼルナッツ	*heezeru nattsu*
heart	心臓	*shinzoo*
herb	ハーブ	*haabu*
herring	ニシン	*nishin*
honey	蜂蜜(ハニー)	*hachimitsu (hanii)*
hot chocolate	ココア	*kokoa*
hot dog	ホットドッグ	*hotto doggu*
ice (cube)	氷	*koori*
ice cream	アイスクリーム	*aisu kuriimu*
iced coffee	アイスコーヒー	*aisu koohii*

iced tea	アイスティー	*aisu tii*
jam	ジャム	*jamu*
Japanese pickled vegetables	漬物	*tsukemono*
Japanese snacks	おつまみ	*otsumami*
Japanese-style curry on rice	カレーライス	*karee raisu*
juice	ジュース	*juusu*
ketchup	ケチャップ	*kechappu*
kiwi	キウィ	*kiui*
lamb	ラム肉	*ramu niku*
leek	ねぎ/葱	*negi*
leg	もも肉	*momo niku*
lemon	レモン	*remon*
lemonade	レモネード	*remoneedo*
lentil	平豆	*hiramame*
lettuce	レタス	*retasu*
lime	ライム	*raimu*
liver	レバー	*rebaa*
lobster	ロブスター	*robusutaa*
mackerel	鯖(サバ)	*saba*

mango	マンゴー *mangoo*
margerine	マーガリン *maagarin*
mayonnaise	マヨネーズ *mayoneezu*
meat	肉 *niku*
melon	メロン *meron*
milk (a carton)	牛乳 *gyuunyuu*
milk (when ordering in a restaurant)	ミルク *miruku*
milkshake	ミルクセーキ *mirukuseeki*
mineral water	ミネラルウォーター *mineraru wootaa*
mint	ミント *minto*
miso (paste made from fermented soybeans)	味噌 *miso*
miso soup	みそ汁 *misoshiru*
MSG (monosodium glutamate)	味の素 *aji no moto*
mushrooms	マッシュルーム *masshuruumu*
mussels	ムール貝 *muuru gai*
mustard	からし *karashi*
mutton	マトン *maton*
noodle	うどん *udon*
buckwheat noodle broth, meat or egg, veg	そば *soba*
wheat-flour noodle broth, meat or egg,veg	うどん *udon*
Chinese noodle broth	ラーメン *raamen*
wheat-flour noodles	そうめん *soomen*
nougat	ヌガー *nugaa*
nuts	ナッツ *nattsu*
oatmeal	オートミール *ootomiiru*
octopus	蛸(タコ) *tako*

olive	オリーブ *oriibu*
olive oil	オリーブオイル *oriibu oiru*
omelet	オムレツ *omuretsu*
onion	玉ねぎ *tamanegi*
orange	オレンジ *orenji*
orange juice	オレンジジュース *orenji juusu*
oregano	オレガノ *oregano*
ox	オックス *okkusu*
oxtail	オックステール *okkusu teeru*
oyster	牡蛎 *kaki*
pancake	パンケーキ *pankeeki*
papaya	パパイヤ *papaiya*
paprika	パプリカ *papurika*
pasta	パスタ *pasuta*
pastry	ペストリー *pesutorii*
peach	桃 *momo*
peanut	ピーナッツ *piinattsu*
pear (Japanese pears)	梨 *nashi*
pea	グリンピース *gurinpiisu*
pecan	ピーカン *piikan*
pepper (vegetable)	ピーマン *pepper*
persimmon	柿 *kaki*
pickle [gherkin]	ピクルス *pikurusu*
pineapple	パイナップル *painappuru*
pizza	ピザ *piza*
plum	プラム *puramu*
pork	豚肉 *buta niku*
potato (Japanese dishes)	馬鈴薯/じゃがいも *bareesho/jagaimo*
potato (Western dishes)	ポテト *poteto*
potato chips [crisps]	ポテトチップ *poteto chippu*

prune	プルーン	*puruun*
pudding	プリン	*purin*
pumpkin	かぼちゃ	*kabocha*
quail	ウズラ	*uzura*
rabbit	ウサギ肉	*usagi niku*
radish	ラディッシュ	*radisshu*
raisin	レーズン	*reezun*
relish	レリッシュ	*rerisshu*
rice	ご飯	*gohan*
rice crackers	煎餅	*senbee*
roast	ロースト	*roosuto*
roast beef	ローストビーフ	*roosuto biifu*
roll	ロールパン	*rooru pan*
rum	ラム酒	*ramu shu*
salad	サラダ	*sarada*
salami	サラミ	*sarami*
salmon	鮭(サケ)	*sake*
salmon roe	いくら	*ikura*
salt	塩	*shio*
sandwich	サンドイッチ	*sandoitchi*
sardine	イワシ	*iwashi*
sauce	ソース	*soosu*
sausage	ソーセージ	*sooseeji*
savory pancakes	お好み焼き	*okonomiyaki*
scallion [spring onion]	ねぎ	*negi*
scallop	帆立貝	*hotate gai*
scotch	スコッチ	*sukotchi*
seafood	魚介類/海鮮料理	*gyokai rui/kaisen ryoori*
seaweed (dried)	海苔	*nori*
sherry	シェリー	*sherii*
shitake mushroom	椎茸(しいたけ)	*shiitake*

shrimp [prawns]	海老	*ebi*
soda	炭酸飲料	*tansan inryoo*
soda water	ソーダ	*sooda*
soup	スープ	*suupu*
soy (sauce)	醤油	*shooyu*
spaghetti	スパゲッティ	*supagetti*
spinach	ほうれん草	*hoorensoo*
squash	かぼちゃ	*kabocha*
squid	いか	*ika*
steak	ステーキ	*suteeki*
strawberry	苺(いちご)	*ichigo*
sugar	砂糖	*satoo*
sweets	甘いもの	*amaimono*
sweet potato	サツマイモ	*satsumaimo*
swordfish	メカジキ	*mekajiki*
syrup	シロップ	*shiroppu*
tangerine	蜜柑(みかん)	*mikan*
tarragon	タラゴン	*taragon*
tea (black)	紅茶	*koocha*
toast	トースト	*toosuto*
thyme	タイム	*taimu*

tofu (soybean curd)	豆腐 *toofu*
tomato	トマト *tomato*
tonic water	トニック *tonikku*
tripe	胃袋 *ibukuro*
trout	鱒(マス) *masu*
truffles	トリュフ *toryufu*
tuna	鮪(マグロ) *maguro*
turkey	七面鳥 *shichimenchoo*
turnip	かぶ *kabu*
vanilla	バニラ *banira*
veal	子牛の肉 *koushinoniku*
vegetable	野菜 *yasai*
venison	鹿の肉 *shika no niku*
vermouth	ベルモット *berumotto*
vodka	ウォッカ *wokka*
vinegar	酢 *su*
water	水 *mizu*
watercress	クレソン *kureson*
watermelon	西瓜(すいか) *suika*
wheat	小麦 *komugi*
wheat noodles	うどん *udon*
whisky	ウイスキー *uisukii*
white radish	大根 *daikon*
whitebait	白子(シラス) *shirasu*
wild boar	猪 *inoshishi*
wine	ワイン *wain*
yogurt	ヨーグルト *yooguruto*
zucchini [courgette]	ズッキーニ *zukkiini*

People

Conversation

ESSENTIAL

Hello.	こんにちは。	*konnichiwa*
How are you?	お元気ですか。	*ogenki desu ka*
Fine, thanks.	はい、おかげさまで。	*hai okage sama de*
Excuse me! (to get attention)	失礼します。	*shitsuree shimasu*
Do you speak English?	英語ができますか。	*eego ga dekimasu ka*
What's your name?	お名前は。	*onamae wa*
My name is...	...です。	*...desu*
Pleased to meet you.	よろしくお願いします。	*yoroshiku onegai shimasu*
Where are you from?	どちらからですか。	*dochira kara desu ka*
I'm from the U.S./U.K.	アメリカ/イギリスからです。	*amerika/igirisu kara desu*
What do you do?	何をしていますか。	*nani o shite imasu ka*
I work for...	...に勤めています。	*...ni tsutomete imasu*
I'm a student.	学生です。	*gakusee desu*
I'm retired.	退職しました。	*taishoku shimashita*
Do you like...?	は好きですか。	*...wa suki desu ka*
Goodbye.	さようなら。	*sayoonara*
See you later.	それではまた。	*sore dewa mata*

Language Difficulties

Do you speak English?	英語ができますか	*eego ga dekimasu ka*
Does anyone here speak English?	英語ができる人はいますか。	*eego ga dekiru hito wa imasu ka*
I don't speak (much) Japanese.	(あまり)日本語ができません。	*(amari) nihongo ga dekimasen*

It is customary in Japan to address people by their last name first, though more recently when meeting foreigners many Japanese will give their surname last. Generally, the suffix-**san** (Mr., Mrs., or Ms.) is used after the last name, so someone with a last name of Honda and a first name of Kenji would be addressed as Honda-**san**. Never use **san** to talk about yourself.

Could you speak more slowly?	ゆっくり言ってくれませんか。 *yukkuri itte kuremasen ka*
Could you repeat that?	もう一度、言ってくれませんか。 *moo ichido itte kuremasen ka*
Excuse me? [Pardon?]	すみません *sumimasen*
What was that?	何ですか。*nan desu ka*
Please write it down.	書いてください。*kaite kudasai*
Can you translate this for me?	訳してください。*yakushite kudasai*
What does this/that mean?	これ/それは、何という意味ですか。 *kore/sore wa nan to yuu imi desu ka*
I understand.	分力、りました。*wakarimashita*

Japanese has three levels of speech: plain, polite and honorific. Which level to use is determined by how well you know the other person, and also by age, social status and situation. Female speakers tend to employ polite speech, and young people often use plain speech. Japanese culture emphasizes respect, so honorific speech is appropriate when a younger person addresses an older person, or a person in an organization or company addresses a superior. Honorific speech is also used when trying to sell goods or services to others. An appropriate greeting for the first meeting between adults is **Hajimemashite**, which literally means 'For the first time'. In subsequent meetings, this changes to **konnichi wa** (during the day) or **konban wa** (in the afternoon), which are still polite. **Yaa** (for men) and **Ara** (for women), both meaning Hi! are only appropriate among friends, in a casual setting.

In this book, you will find polite and honorific speech style.

| I don't understand. | 分かりません。 *wakarimasen* |
| Do you understand? | 分力、り·ます力、。 *wakarimasu ka* |

Making Friends

Hello.	こんにちは *konnichi wa*
Pleased to meet you!	初めまして。 *hajimemashite*
Good morning.	おはようございます。 *ohayoo gozaimasu*
Good afternoon.	こんにちは。 *konnichi wa*
Good evening.	こんばんは。 *konban wa*
My name is...	...です。 *...desu*
What's your name?	お名前は。 *onamae wa*
I'd like to introduce you to...	...さんをご紹介します *...san o goshookai shimasu*

YOU MAY SEE...

英語が少ししかできません。 *eego ga sukoshi shika dekimasen*	I only speak a little English.
英語はできません。 *eego wa dekimasen*	I don't speak English.

Nice to meet you.	よろしくお願いします。 *yoroshiku onegai shimasu*
How are you?	お元気ですか。 *ogenki desu ka*
Fine, thanks.	はい、おかげさまで。 *hai, okage sama de.*
And you?	いかがですか。 *ikaga desu ka*

Travel Talk

I'm here...	...で来ました。 *...dekimashita*
on business	仕事 *shigoto*
on vacation [holiday]	観光[休暇] *kankoo [kyuuka]*
studying	研究 *kenkyuu*
I'm staying for...	...間、滞在しています。 *...kan taizai shiteimasu*
I've been here...	...前に、来ました。 *...mae ni kimashita*
a day	日 *nichi/hi*
a week	週 *shuu*

a month	月 *tsuki*
Where are you from?	どちらからですか。*dochira kara desu ka*
I'm from...	...から来ました。*...kara kimashita*

For Numbers, see page 155.

Personal

Who are you with?	どなたとご一緒ですか。*donata to goissho desu ka*
I'm on my own.	一人です。*hitori desu*
I'm with my...	...と一緒です。*...to issho desu*
husband/wife	主人/家内 *shujin/kanai*
boyfriend/girlfriend	ボーイフレンド/ガールフレンド *booifurendo/gaarufurendo*
friend(s)	友人 *yuujin*
colleague(s)	同僚 *dooryoo*
When's your birthday?	誕生日はいつですか。*tanjoobi wa itsu desu ka*
How old are you?	何歳ですか。*nansai desu ka*
I'm...	...歳です。*...sai desu*
Are you married?	結婚していますか。*kekkon shite imasu ka*
I'm...	私は...*watashi wa...*
single	ひとりです。*hitori desu*
in a relationship	付き合っています。*tsukiatte imasu*
engaged	...婚約中です。*kon-yaku chuu desu*
married	結婚しています。*kekkon shite imasu*
divorced	離婚しました。*rikon shimashita*
separated	別居中です。*bekkyo chuu desu*
I'm widowed.	妻/夫を亡くしました。*tsuma f / otto m o nakushimashita*
Do you have children/ grandchildren?	お子さん/お孫さんがいますか。*okosan/omagosan ga imasu ka*

Work & School

What do you do?	（お仕事は）何をしていますか。
	(oshigoto wa)nani o shite imasu ka
What are you studying?	何を勉強していますか。
	nani o benkyoo shite imasu ka
I'm studying...	...を勉強しています。 *...o benkyoo shite imasu*
I work full time/part time.	フルタイム/パートタイムです。
	furu/paato taimu desu
I'm between jobs.	求職中です。 *kyuushoku chuu desu*
I work at home.	自宅で仕事をしています。
	jitaku de shigoto o shiteimasu
Who do you work for?	どちらにお勤めですか。
	dochira ni otsutome desu ka
I work for...	...に勤めています。 *...ni tsutomete imasu*
Here's my business card.	名刺をどうぞ。 *meeshi o doozo*

Weather

What's the weather forecast for tomorrow?	明日の予報は何ですか。 *ashita no yohoo wa nan desu ka*
What beautiful/terrible weather!	なんてきれいな/いやな天気なんでしょう。 *nante kireina/iyana tenki nan deshoo*
It's cool/warm.	涼しい/暖かいです。 *suzushii/atatakai desu*
It's rainy/sunny.	雨/晴れです。 *ame/hare desu*
It's snowy/icy.	雪が降って/凍っています。
	yuki ga futte/kootte imasu
Do I need a jacket/an umbrella?	上着/傘がいりますか。 *uwagi/kasa ga irimasu ka*

For Conversion Tables, see page 162.

Romance

ESSENTIAL

Would you like to go out for a drink/meal?	飲み物/食事はいかがですか。 *nomimono/ shokuji wa ikaga desu ka*
What are your plans for tonight/tomorrow?	今晩/明日予定はありますか。 *konban/ashita yotee wa arimasu ka*
Can I have your number?	電話番号を教えてくれませんか。 *denwa bangoo o oshiete kuremasen ka*
Can I join you?	ご一緒してもいいですか。 *goissho shitemo ii desu ka*
Can I buy you a drink?	一杯おごらせてください。 *ippai ogorasete kudasai*
I like you.	あなたが気に入りました。 *anata ga kini irimashita*
I love you.	あなたが好きです。 *anata ga suki desu*

The Dating Game

Would you like to...?	行きませんか。 *...ikimasen ka*
go out for coffee	コーヒーを飲みに *koohii o nomi ni*
go for a drink	飲みに *nomi ni*
go out for a meal	食事に *shokuji ni*
What are your for...?	...予定はありますか。 *...yotee wa arimasu ka*
today	今日 *kyoo*
tonight	今晩 *konban*
tomorrow	明日 *ashita*
this weekend	今週末 *konshuumatsu*
Where would you like to go?	どこに行きましょうか。 *doko ni ikimashoo ka*

I'd like to go to…	…に行きたいです。… ni ikitai desu
Do you like…?	…は好きですか。… wa suki desu ka
Can I have your number/e-mail ?	電話番号/Eメールアドレスを教えてくれませんか。denwabangoo/iimeeru adoresu o oshiete kuremasen ka
Can I join you?	ご一緒してもいいですか。 goissho shitemo ii desu ka
You're very attractive.	あなたはとても魅力的ですね。 anata wa totemo miryokuteki desu ne
Let's go somewhere quieter.	もっと静かなところへ行きましょう。 motto shizukana tokoro e ikimasshoo

For Communications, see page 48.

Accepting & Rejecting

I'd love to.	喜んで yorokonde
Where should we meet?	どこで待ち合わせましょうか。doko de machiawasemashoo ka
I'll meet you at the bar/your hotel.	バー/ホテルで会いましょう。 baa/hoteru de aimashoo
I'll come by at…	…に来ます。… ni kimasu
What's your address?	住所は? juusho wa

Thank you, but I'm busy.	申し訳ありませんが、約束があります。 *mooshiwake arimasen ga yakusoku ga arimasu*
I'm not interested.	興味がありません。*kyuoomi ga arimasen*
Leave me alone.	構わないでください。*kamawanaide kudasai*
Stop bothering me!	邪魔するのはやめてください。 *jama suru nowa yamete kudasai*

Getting Intimate

Can I hug/kiss you?	抱き締めても/キスしてもいいですか。 *dakishimetemo/kisushitemo ii desu ka*
Yes.	はい *hai*
No.	いいえ *iie*
Stop!	やめて! *yamete*

Sexual Preferences

Are you gay?	あなたはゲイですか。*anata wa gee desu ka*
I'm...	私は…です。*watashi wa . . . desu*
heterosexual	ヘテロ *hetero*
homosexual	ホモ *homo*
bisexual	バイ *bai*
Do you like men/ women ?	男性/女性が好きですか。 *dansei/josei ga suki desu ka*

For Grammar, see page 152.

Leisure Time

Sightseeing

ESSENTIAL

Where's the tourist information office?	観光案内所はどこですか。 *kankoo annaijo wa doko desu ka*
What are the main points of interest?	観光名所はどこですか。 *kankoo meesho wa doko desu ka*
Do you have tours in English?	英語のツアーがありますか。 *eego no tsuaa ga arimasu ka*
Could I have a map/guide please?	地図/案内書をください。 *chizu/annaisho o kudasai*

The Japan National Tourist Organization (JNTO) operates Tourist Information Centers (TIC) in Japan and overseas. These centers provide a wealth of information, including free maps, brochures, tour itineraries and advice on travel to and within Japan. They will give advice on the 'goodwill guide', a free service, as well as professional guide services. In Tokyo, at Tokyo and Shinjuku rail stations, you will find special centers called Information for Foreigners (**gaikokujin annai jo**) providing foreigners with information on sightseeing, travel, living in Tokyo and much more.

Tourist Information

Can you recommend...?	...はありますか。*... wa arimasu ka*
a boat trip	遊覧船 *yuuransen*
an excursion	遊覧旅行 *yuuran ryokoo*

| a sightseeing tour | 観光ツアー *kankoo tsuaa* |
| Do you have any information on...? | ...の案内はありますか。...*no annai wa arimasu ka* |

On Tour

I'd like to go on the tour to...	...へのツアーに参加したいんですが。...*e no tsuaa ni sanka shitain desu ga*
When's the next tour?	英語のツアーがありますか。 *sugi no tsuaa wa itsu desu ka*
Are there tours in English?	英語のツアーがありますか。 *eego no tsuaa ga arimasu ka*
Is there an English-speaking guide/audio guide?	英語のガイド / オーディオがありますか。 *eego no gaido/oodio ga arimasu ka*
What time do we leave/return?	何時に出ますか/ 戻りますか。 *nanji ni demasu ka/modorimasu ka*
We'd like to have a look at the...	...を見たいんですが。...*o mitain desu ga*
Can we stop here...?	...ここで止まれますか。...*koko de tomaremasu ka*
to take photographs	写真を撮りたいんですが、*shashin o toritain desu ga*
to buy souvenirs	お土産を買いたいんですが、 *omiyage o kaitain desu ga*
to use the bathrooms [toilets]	トイレに行きたいんですが、*toire ni ikitain desu ga*
Is there access for the disabled?	身体障害者は入れますか。 *shintai shogaisha wa hairemasu ka*

For Tickets, see page 20.

Seeing the Sights

Where is the...?	...はどこですか。...*wa doko desu ka*
art gallery	美術館 *bijutsukan*
battle site	戦場跡 *senjoo ato*

botanical garden	植物園 *shokubutsuen*
Buddhist temple	お寺 *otera*
castle	お城 *oshiro*
castle remains	城跡 *shiro ato*
cemetery	墓地 *bochi*
church	教会 *kyookai*
downtown area	繁華街 *hankagai*
fountain	噴水 *funsui*
historic site	史跡 *shiseki*
(war) memorial	(戦争) 記念碑 *(sensoo) kinen hi*
museum	博物館 *hakubutsukan*
five-story [storey] pagoda	五重塔 *gojuu no too*
Imperial palace	皇居 *kookyo*
Where is the...?	...はどこですか。*...wa doko desu ka*
park	公園 *kooen*
parliament building	国会議事堂 *kokkai gijidoo*
Shinto shrine	神社 *jinja*
shopping area	商店街 *shootengai*
statue	銅像 *doozoo*
theater [theatre]	劇場 *gekijoo*
town hall	市役所 *shiyakusho*

Can you show me on the map?	この地図で教えてください。
	kono chizu de oshiete kudasai
It's…	…ですね。 *…desu ne*
amazing	すごい *sugoi*
beautiful	美しい *utsukushii*
boring	つまらない *tsumaranai*
interesting	おもしろい *omoshiroi*
magnificent	立派 *rippa*
romantic	ロマンチック *romanchikku*
strange	変 *hen*
superb	素晴らしい *subarashii*
terrible	ひどい *hidoi*
ugly	醜い *minikui*
I like it./I don't like it.	好きです/好きではありません。
	suki desu/dewa arimasen

For Asking Directions, see page 35.

Religious Sites

Where's…?	…はどこですか。 *…wa doko desu ka*
the cathedral	大聖堂 *daiseedoo*
the Catholic/ Protestant church	カトリック/プロテスタント教会 *katorikku/purotesutanto kyookai*
the mosque	回教寺院 *kaikyoo jiin*
the Shinto shrine	神社 *jinja*
the synagogue	ユダヤ教会堂 *yudaya kyookaidoo*
the Buddhist/ Zen temple	寺/禅寺 *tera/zendera*
What time is mass/ the service?	ミサ / 礼拝 は何時ですか。 *misa/reehai wa nanji desu ka*

Shopping

ESSENTIAL

Where is the shopping center?	ショッピングセンターはどこですか。 *shoppinngu sentaa wa doko desu ka*
I'm just looking.	ちょっと見ているだけです。 *chotto miteiru dake desu*
Can you help me?	ちょっと、お願いします。 *chotto onegai shimasu*
I'm being helped.	大丈夫です。 *daijoobu desu*
How much?	いくらですか。 *ikura desu ka*
That one.	それ *sore*
That's all, thanks.	それで結構です。 *sorede kekkoo desu*
Where can I pay?	どこで払うんですか。 *doko de haraun desu ka*
I'll pay in cash/by credit card.	現金/(クレジット)カードで払います。 *genkin/(kurejitto) kaado de haraimasu*
A receipt, please.	レシートをお願いします。 *reshiito o onegai shimasu*

Japanese people usually shop at department stores for clothing and household items. You will not be able to bargain at department stores, which tend to sell more expensive items. There are two large, upscale shopping centers, Roppongi Hills and Omote Sando Hills, in Tokyo. If you want to find bargain items, visit a flea market at the neighborhood temple or town square, where vendors sell used kimonos, household items or antiques. If you are interested in small electronic items such as audio-video equipment, home appliances, computers, computer games or anime and anime related characters, visit Akihabara in Tokyo. Several blocks surrounding the Akihabara Station are filled with stores selling all kinds of items.

At the Shops

Where's the...?	...はどこですか。...wa doko desu ka
antiques store	骨董品店 kottoohinten
bakery	パン屋 pan ya
bank	銀行 ginkoo
bookstore	本屋 hon ya
clothing store	洋服屋 yoofukuya
delicatessen	デリカテッセン derikatessen
department store	デパート depaato
health food store	健康食品店 kenkoo shokuhin ten
jeweler	宝石店 hooseki ten
liquor store [off-licence]	酒屋 sakaya
market	マーケット maaketto
pastry shop	ケーキ屋 keekiya
pharmacy [chemist]	薬局 yakkyoku
produce [grocery] store	食料品店 shokuryoohin ten
shoe store	靴屋 kutsuya
shopping mall [shopping centre]	ショッピングセンター shoppinngu sentaa

the souvenir store	お土産屋 *omiyageya*
the supermarket	スーパー *suupaa*
the tobacconist	タバコ屋 *tabakoya*
the toy store	おもちゃ屋 *omochaya*

Ask an Assistant

What are the opening hours?	開店時間は何時ですか。 *kaiten jikan wa nanji desu ka*
Where is/are...?	...はどこですか。*...wa doko desu ka*
the cashier [cash desk]	会計 *kaikee*
the escalator	エスカレーター *esukareetaa*
the elevator [lift]	エレベーター *erebeetaa*
the fitting room	試着室 *shichakushitsu*
the store directory [guide]	店内の案内 *tennai no annai*
Can you help me?	ちょっと、お願いします。*chotto onegai shimasu*
I'm just looking.	ちょっと見ているだけです。 *chotto miteiru dake desu*
I'm being helped.	大丈夫です。*daijoobu desu*
Do you have...?	...は、ありますか。*...wa arimasu ka*

YOU MAY HEAR...

いらっしゃいませ。*irasshaimase*	Welcome!
少々お待ちください。 *shooshoo omachi kudasai*	One moment.
何がよろしいですか。 *nani ga yoroshii desu ka*	What would you like?
他に何かございますか。 *hoka ni nanika gozaimasu ka*	Anything else?

YOU MAY SEE...

開店/閉店 *kaiten/heeten*	open/closed	
昼食のため休業中	closed for lunch	
chuusyoku no tame kyuugyoo chuu		
試着室 *shichakushitsu*	fitting room	
お会計 *okaikei*	cashier	
現金のみ *genkin nomi*	cash only	
クレジットカードも受け付けます	credit cards	
kurejitto kaado mo uketsuke masu	accepted	
営業時間 *eigyoo jikan*	business hours	
出口 *deguchi*	exit	

Could you show me...?	…を見せてください。*…o misete kudasai*
Can you ship/wrap it?	届けて/包装してください。 *todokete/hoosoo shite kudasai*
How much?	いくらですか。*ikura desu ka*
That's all, thanks.	それで全部です。*sore de zenbu desu*

For Clothing, see page 114.

For Meals & Cooking, see page 64.

For Souvenirs, see page 120.

Personal Preferences

I'd like something...	…のが欲しいんですが。*…no ga hoshiin desu ga*
cheap/expensive	安い/高い *yasui/takai*
larger/smaller	もっと大きい/小さい *motto ookii/chiisai*
from this region	この地方から *kono chihoo kara*
Is it real?	本物ですか。*honmono desu ka*
Could you show me this/that?	これ/それを見せてください。 *kore/sore o misete kudasai*

That's not quite what I want.	私が思っているのと少し違うんですが。
	watashi ga omotte iru noto sukoshi chigaun desu ga
No, I don't like it.	あまり好きではありません。
	amari suki dewa arimasen
That's too expensive.	高すぎます。*taka sugimasu*
I'd like to think about it.	考えさせてください。*kangae sasete kudasai*
I'll take it.	それにします。*sore ni shimasu*

Paying & Bargaining

How much?	いくらですか。*ikura desu ka*
I'll pay.	…で払います。*...de haraimasu*
in cash	現金 *genkin*
by credit card	(クレジット) カード *(kurejitto) kaado*
by traveler's check [cheque]	トラベラーズチェック *toraberaazu chekku*
A receipt, please.	レシートをお願いします。
	reshiito o onegai shimasu
That's too much.	高すぎます。*taka sugimasu*
I'll give you…	…でどうですか。*...de doo desu ka*
I only have…yen.	…円しかありません。*...en shika arimasen*
Is that your best price?	もっと安くなりませんか。
	motto yasuku narimasen ka
Can you give me a discount?	割引してくれませんか。
	waribiki shite kuremasen ka

For Numbers, see page 155.

Visitors to Japan can use the international credit cards at most stores, however, withdrawing cash using your credit card is limited to a small number of ATMs.

YOU MAY HEAR...

お支払いはどうなさいますか。
oshiharai wa doo nasaimasu ka

How are you paying?

このカードで承認が得られませんでした。
kono kaado de shoonin ga eraremasen deshita

This transaction has not been approved.

他に身分証明はお持ちですか
hoka ni mibun shoomeisho wa omochi desu ka

May I have additional identification?

現金でお願し、します。
genkin de onegai shimasu

Cash only, please.

小銭はございますか。
kozeni wa gozaimasu ka

Do you have any smaller change?

Making a Complaint

I'd like...	...ですが 。 ...*desu ga*	
to exchange this	交換したいん	*kookan shitain*
to return this	返品したいん	*henpin shitain*
a refund	返金してもらいたいん	*henkin shite moraitain*
to see the manager	マネージャーに会いたいん	*maneejaa ni aitain*

Services

Can you recommend...?	いい...はありますか。 *ii...wa arimasu ka*	
a barber	床屋	*tokoya*
a dry cleaner	ドライクリーニング店	*dorai kuriiningu ten*
a hairdresser	美容院	*biyooin*
a laundromat [launderette]	コインランドリー	*koin randorii*
a nail salon	ネイルサロン	*neeru saron*
a spa	スパ	*supa*
a travel agency	旅行代理店	*ryokoo dairiten*
Can you...this?	...できますか。 *...dekimasu ka*	

alter	仕立て直し *shitatenaoshi*
clean	洗濯 *sentaku*
mend	修繕 *shuuzen*
press	プレス *puresu*
When will it be ready?	いつできますか。*itsu dekimasu ka*

Hair & Beauty

I'd like...	…をお願いしたいんですが。
	...o onegaishitain desu ga
an appointment for today/tomorrow	今日/明日の予約 *kyoo/ashita no yoyaku*
some color	カラー *karaa*
some highlights	ハイライト *hairaito*
my hair styled	スタイル *sutairu*
a haircut	カット *katto*
I'd like a trim.	そろえてもらいたいんですが。
	soroete moraitain desu ga
Don't cut it too short.	切りすぎないでください。*kiri suginai de kudasai*
Shorter here.	ここをもう少し短くして下さい。
	koko o moo sukoshi mijikaku shite kudasai
I'd like.	…をお願いしたいんですが。*o onegai shitain desuga*
an eyebrow/bikini wax	眉毛/ビキニワックス
	mayuge/bikini wakkusu
a facial	フエーシヤノレ *feesharu*
a manicure	マニキュア *manikyua*
pedicure	ペディキュア *pedikyua*
a (sports) massage	(スポーツ)マッサージ *supootsu massaaji*
Do you do...?	…をしますか。*...o shimasu ka*
acupuncture	鍼 *hari*
aromatherapy	アロマセラピー *aromaserapii*
oxygen treatment	酸素治療 *sanso chiryoo*
Is there a sauna?	サウナがありますか。*sauna ga arimasu ka*

For relaxation in a traditional setting, visit one of many hot springs throughout Japan. You will find special facilities at hotels and Japanese inns near hot spring areas. A hot spring is enjoyed just like a bath: traditionally no bathing suit is worn, and there are separate areas for men and women. Sometimes you will find a smaller area for family use. In addition to the hot springs, there are many day spas in the cities, and hotel and resort spas are also available. Prices are comparable to the west, but tipping is not expected.

Antiques

How old is this?	どのくらい古いですか。 *dono kurai furui desu ka*
Do you have anything of the...era?	…時代のものはありますか。 *...jidai no mono wa arimasu ka*
Will I have problems with customs?	税関で問題になりますか。 *zeekan de mondai ni narimasu ka*
Is there a certificate of authenticity?	鑑定書はありますか。*kanteesho wa arimasu ka*

Clothing

I'd like.	…が欲しいんですが。*...ga hoshiin desu ga*
Can I try this on?	これを試着できますか。 *kore o shichaku dekimasu ka*
It doesn't fit.	身体に合いません。*karada ni aimasen*
It's too...	…すぎます。*...sugimasu*
big	大き *ooki*
small	小さ *chiisa*
short	短 *mijika*
long	長 *naga*

Do you have this in size...?	これで…サイズのはありますか。
	korede... saizu no wa arimasu ka
Do you have this in a bigger/smaller size?	もう少し大きい/小さいのがありますか。
	moo sukoshi ookii/chiisai no ga arimasu ka

For Numbers, see page 155.

YOU MAY HEAR...

とてもよくお似合いです。　　　That looks great on you.
totemo yoku oniai desu

いかがですか。*ikaga desu ka*　　How does it fit?

お客様に合うサイズがありません。　We don't have your size.
okyaku sama ni au saizu ga arima sen

YOU MAY SEE...

紳士服	men's clothing
婦人服	women's clothing
子供服	children's clothing

Colors

I'm looking for something in...	...のを探しているんですが。
	...no o sagashite irun desu ga
beige	ベージュ *beeju*
black	黒い *kuroi*
blue	ブルー *buruu*
brown	茶色 *chairo*
green	グリーン *guriin*
gray [grey]	グレー *guree*
orange	オレンジ色 *orenji iro*
pink	ピンク *pinku*
purple	紫 *murasaki*
red	赤い *akai*
white	白い *shiroi*
yellow	黄色 *kiiro*

Clothes & Accessories

backpack	リュックサック *ryukkusakku*
belt	ベルト *beruto*
bikini	ビキニ *bikini*
blouse	ブラウス *burausu*
bra	ブラジャー *burajaa*
coat	コート *kooto*
dress	ワンピース *wanpiisu*
hat	帽子 *booshi*
jacket	上着 *uwagi*
jeans	ジーパン *jiipan*
pajamas	パジャマ *pajama*
panties	パンティー（女性用の下着）
(women's underwear)	*pantii (joseiyoo no shitagi)*
pants [trousers]	ズボン *zubon*

panty hose [tights]	パンスト *pansuto*
purse [handbag]	ハンドバッグ *handobaggu*
raincoat	レインコート *einkooto*
scarf	スカーフ *sukaafu*
shirt (men's)	ワイシャツ *waishatsu*
shorts	半ズボン *hanzubon*
skirt	スカート *sukaato*
socks	靴下 *kutsushita*
suit	スーツ *suutsu*
sunglasses	サングラス *sangurasu*
sweater	セーター *seetaa*
sweatshirt	トレーナー *toreenaa*
swimsuit	水着 *mizugi*
T-shirt	Tシャツ *tii shatsu*
tie	ネクタイ *nekutai*
underpants	ノベンツ *pantsu*

Fabric

I'd like...	...が欲しいんですが。...*ga hoshiin desu ga*
cotton	綿/コットン *men/kotton*
denim	デニム *denimu*
lace	レース *reesu*
leather	革 *kawa*
linen	麻 *asa*
silk	絹 *kinu*
wool	ウール *uuru*
Is it machine washable?	洗濯機で洗えますか。*sentakuki de araemasu ka*

Shoes

I'd like…	…が欲しいんですが。	…ga hoshiin desu ga
high-heeled/flat shoes.	ハイヒール/平らな靴	haihiiru/taira na kutsu
boots	ブーツ	buutsu
loafers	ローファー	roofaa
sandals	サンダル	sandaru
shoes	靴	kutsu
slippers	スリッパ	surippa
sneakers	スニーカー	suniikaa
In size…	サイズ…の	saizu…no

For Numbers, see page 155.

Sizes

small (S)	小	shoo
medium (M)	中	chuu
large (L)	大	dai
extra large (XL)	特大	tokudai
petite	プチサイズ	puchi saizu
plus size	大きいサイズ	ookii saizu

Newsagent & Tobacconist

Do you sell English-language books/newspapers?	英語の本/新聞はありますか。	*eego no hon/shinbun wa arimasu ka*
I'd like...	...が欲しいんですが。	*...ga hoshiin desu ga*
candy [sweets]	キャンデー	*kyandee*
chewing gum	ガム	*gamu*
a chocolate bar	チョコレート	*chokoreeto*
cigars	葉巻	*hamaki*
a pack/carton of cigarettes	煙草一箱/一カートン	*tabako hitohako/ichi kaaton*
a lighter	ライター	*raitaa*
a magazine	雑誌	*zasshi*
matches	マッチ	*matchi*
a newspaper	新聞	*shinbun*
a pen	ボールペン	*boorupen*
a postcard	絵葉書	*ehagaki*
a road/town map of...	...の道路/市街地図	*...no dooro/shigai chizu*
stamps	切手	*kitte*

Photography

I'm looking for a(n)...camera.	...カメラを探しているんですが。	*...kamera o sagashite irun desu ga*
automatic	オートマチック	*ootomachikku*
digital	デジタル	*dejitaru*
disposable	使い捨て	*tsukaisute*
I'd like...	...が欲しいんですが。	*...ga hoshiin desu ga*
a battery	電池	*denchi*
digital prints	デジタルカメラプリント	*dejitaru kamera purinto*

119

a memory card	メモリーカード *memorii kaado*
Can I print digital photos here?	デジタル写真をプリントできますか。 *dejitaru shashin o purinto dekimasu ka*

Souvenirs

dolls	人形 *ningyoo*
electrical goods	電気製品 *denki seehin*
fans	扇子 *sensu*
cloth wrap traditionally used as a handbag	風呂敷 *furoshiki*
handcrafts	工芸品 *koogeehin*
kimono	着物 *kimono*
lacquerware	漆器 *shikki*
ornaments	装飾品 *sooshokuhin*
paper crafts	紙細工 *kami zaiku*
pearls	真珠 *shinju*
porcelain	磁器 *jiki*
pottery	焼き物 *yakimono*
prints	版画 *hanga*
sake (rice wine)	日本酒 *nihonshu*
woodblock prints	木版 *mokuhan*
yukata (cotton bathrobe)	浴衣 *yukata*
Can I see this/that?	これ/それをお願いします。 *kore/sore o onegai shimasu*
It's the one in the window/display case.	ショーウインドー/ケースにあるのです。 *shoouindoo/keesu ni aru no desu*
I'd like.	…が欲しいんですが。 *. . . ga hoshiin desu ga*
a battery	電池 *denchi*
a bracelet	ブレスレット *buresuretto*
a brooch	ブローチ *buroochi*

120

earrings	イヤリング *iyaringu*
a necklace	ネックレス *nekkuresu*
a ring	指輪/リング *yubiwa/ringu*
a watch	腕時計 *ude dokee*
I'd like...	...が欲しいんですが。*...ga hoshiin desu ga*
copper	銅 *doo*
crystal (quartz)	水晶 *suishoo*
diamonds	ダイアモンド *daiamondo*
white/yellow gold	プラチナ/金 *purachina/kin*
pearls	真珠 *shinju*
pewter	ピューター *pyuutaa*
platinum	プラチナ *purachina*
sterling silver	純銀 *jungin*
Is this real?	本物ですか。*honmono desu ka*
Can you engrave it?	...を彫り込んでください。*...o horikonde kudasai*

You will have no difficulty finding any number of souvenirs and presents to take home. There is something for everybody and in every price range. If you are buying electrical goods, remember that Japan uses 100 volts and that television/video systems may not be compatible.

Different regions have their own specialties: you'll find pottery in Mashiko (north of Tokyo), Bizen (a specific type of pottery) in Okayama and lacquer-ware (called shikki) in Aizu (in Fukushima prefecture), Wajima (in Ishikawa prefecture) and Hida Takayama (in Gifu prefecture). You may also be interested in bamboo products, which are produced throughout Japan.

Sport & Leisure

ESSENTIAL

When's the game?	試合はいつですか。 *shiai wa itsu desu ka*
Where's…?	…はどこですか。 *…wa doko desu ka*
the beach	ビーチ *biichi*
the park	公園 *kooen*
the pool	プール *puuru*
Is it safe to swim/dive here?	ここで泳いでも/飛び込んでも大丈夫ですか。 *kokode oyoidemo/tobikondemo daijoobu desu ka*
Can I rent [hire] golf clubs?	ゴルフクラブを借りたいんですが。 *gorufu kurabu o karitain desu ga*
How much per hour?	料金は1時間いくらですか。 *ryookin wa ichijikan ikura desu ka*
How much per round? (when hiring court)	1試合につきいくらですか。 *hitoshiai ni tsuki ikura desuka*
How far is it to…?	…まで、どのくらいありますか。 *…made dono kurai arimasu ka*
Can you show me on the map?	この地図で教えてください。 *kono chizu de oshiete kudasai*

Watching Sport

When's…?	…はいつですか。 *…wa itsu desu ka*
the basketball game	バスケットボール *basuketto booru no shiai*
the baseball game	野球の試合 *yakyuu no shiai*
the boxing match	ボクシングの試合 *bokushingu no shiai*
the cycling race	自転車レース *jitensha reesu*
the golf tournament	ゴノレフトーナメント *gorufu toonamento*
the soccer game	サッカーの試合 *sakkaa no shiai*
the tennis match	テニスの試合 *tenisu no shiai*

the volleyball game	バレーボールの試合 *bareebooru no shiai*
Which teams are playing?	どのチームが出ますか。*dono chiimu ga demasu ka*
Where's...?	…はどこですか。*...wa doko desu ka*
the horsetrack	競馬場 *keebajoo*
the racetrack	競馬場 *keebajoo*
the stadium	スタジアム *sutajiamu*
Where can I place a bet?	どこで賭け金を払いますか。*doko de kakekin o haraimasu ka*

Most sports that are popular in the West — such as golf, tennis, football, basketball, etc. — are also popular in Japan. Many cities have martial arts halls in which you can watch kendoo, juudoo, aikidoo and karate. Japan's real national sport is sumoo (wrestling). This is an ancient, highly ritualized sport providing a true spectacle. There are six tournaments a year, each lasting 15 days. These are held in January, May, and September in Tokyo; in March in Osaka; July in Nagoya; November in Fukuoka. Skiing is also very popular in this mountainous country, and there are numerous ski resorts. It is best to reserve ski accommodations before you leave.

Playing Sport

Where's...?	...はどこですか。...wa doko desu ka
the golf course	ゴルフ場 gorufujoo
the gym	スポーツジム supootsu jimu
the park	公園 kooen
the tennis courts	テニスコート tenisu kooto
How much per...	料金は...いくらですか。 ryookin wa ...ikura desu ka
day	日 nichi/hi
hour	時間 jikan
game	試合 shiai
round	ラウンド raundo
Can I rent [hire]...?	...を借りられますか。...o kariraremasu ka
golf clubs	クラブ kurabu
equipment	道具 doogu
a racket	ラケット raketto

At the Beach/Pool

Where's the beach/pool?	ビーチ/プールはどこですか。 biichi/puuru wa doko desu ka
Is there...?	...はありますか。...wa arimasu ka
a kiddie pool	子供用のプール kodomo yoo no puuru
an indoor/outdoor pool	屋内/屋外プール okunai/okugai puuru
a lifeguard	プール監視員 puuru kanshiin
Is it safe...?	...大丈夫ですか。...daijoobu desu ka
to swim	泳いでも oyoidemo
to dive	飛び込んでも tobikondemo
for children	子供に kodomo ni
I want to rent [hire]...	...を借りたいんですが。...o karitain desu ga
a deck chair	デッキチェア dekki chea

diving equipment	スキューバダイビング用具
	sukyuuba daibingu yoogu
a jet-ski	ジェットスキー *jetto sukii*
a motorboat	モーターボート *mootaa booto*
a rowboat	ボート *booto*
snorkeling equipment	シュノーケル *shunookeru*
a surfboard	サーフボード *saafuboodo*
a towel	タオル *taoru*
an umbrella	パラソル *parasoru*
water skis	水上スキー *suijoo sukii*
a windsurfer	ウインドサーフィン *uindo saafin*
For…hours.	…時間 *…jikan*

Beaches close to Tokyo and Osaka can be very crowded in the summer, and until September 1, when summer officially ends. Okinawa, the Amakusa Islands, the Yaeyama Islands are good for snorkeling and scuba diving.

Winter Sports

A lift pass for a day/five days, please.	一日/五日分のリフト券、お願いします。
	ichinichi/itsuka bun no rifutoken onegai shimasu
I want to rent [hire]…	…を借りたいんですが。 *…o karitain desu ga*
boots	スキー靴 *sukii gutsu*
a helmet	ヘルメット *herumetto*
poles	ストック *sutokku*
skis	スキー *sukii*
a snowboard	スノーボード *sunoo boodo*
snowshoes	スノーシューズ *sunooshuuzu*

These are too big/small.	大き/小さすぎます。	*ooki/chiisa sugimasu*
Are there lessons?	レッスンがありますか	*ressun ga arimasu ka*
I'm a beginner.	初心者です。	*shoshinsha desu*
I'm experienced.	経験者です。	*keekensha desu*
A trail [piste] map, please.	ゲレンデマップ、お願いします。	*gerende mappu onegai shimasu*

YOU MAY SEE...

ケーブルカー	cable car
リフト	chair lift
初心者	novice
中級	intermediate
上級	expert
コーズ閉鎖中	trail [piste] closed

You will find opportunities for both downhill and cross-country skiing in Japan. Many travelers choose to combine skiing with the delights of a **ryokan** or **minshuku** (traditional Japanese guest houses) offering a hot spa.

Out in the Country

I'd like a map of...	...の地図をください。	*...no chizu o kudasai*
this region	この地域	*kono chiiki*
the walking routes	ハイキングコース	*haikingu koosu*
bike routes	サイクリングコース	*saikuringu koosu*
the trails	ハイキング	*haikingu*

Is it easy/difficult?	やさしい/難しいですか。
	yasashii/muzukashii desu ka
Is it far/steep?	遠い/急斜面ですか。*tooi/kyuushamen desu ka*
How far is it to…?	…まで、どのくらいありますか。
	…made dono kurai arimasu ka
Can you show me on the map?	この地図で教えてください。
	kono chizu de oshiete kudasai
I'm lost.	道に迷いました。*michi ni mayoimashita*
Where's the…?	…はどこですか。*…wa doko desu ka*
bridge	橋 *hashi*
cave	洞窟 *dookutsu*
canal	運河 *unga*
cliff	崖 *gake*
farmhouse	農家 *nooka*
field	野原 *nohara*
forest	森 *mori*
hill	丘 *oka*
island	島 *shima*
lake	湖 *mizuumi*
mountain	山 *yama*
mountain pass	山道 *yama michi*
mountain range	山脈 *sanmyaku*
nature reserve	自然保護区域 *shizen hogo kuiki*
panorama	展望 *tenboo*
park	公園 *kooen*
peak	山頂 *sanchoo*
plain	平野 *heeya*
pond	池 *ike*
rapids	急流 *kyuuryuu*
river	川 *kawa*
hot spring	温泉 *onsen*

stream	小川 *ogawa*
valley	谷間 *tanima*
viewpoint	展望台 *tenboo dai*
village	村 *mura*
waterfall	滝 *taki*
wood	林 *hayashi*

Going Out

ESSENTIAL

What is there to do in the evenings?	夜は 何がありますか。 *yoru wa nani ga arimasu ka*
Do you have a program of events?	催し物のプログラムがありますか。 *moyooshimono no puroguramu gaarimasu ka*
What's playing at the movies [cinema] tonight?	今晩、どんな映画をやっていますか。 *konban donna eega o yatte imasu ka*
Where's...?	...はどこですか。*...wa doko desu ka*
the downtown area	繁華街 *hankagai*
the bar	バー *baa*
the dance club	ディスコ *disuko*
Is there a cover charge?	カバーチャージはありますか。 *kabaa chaaji wa arimasu ka*

Entertainment

Can you recommend...?	...はありますか。*...wa arimasu ka*
a concert	コンサート *konsaato*
a movie	映画 *eega*

an opera	オペラ *opera*
a play	芝居 *shibai*
When does it start/ end?	いつ始まりますか/終わりますか。 *itsu hajimarimasu ka/owarimasu ka*
What's the dress code?	服装規定がありますか。*fukusoo kitei ga arimasu ka*
I like ...	...が好きです。*... ga suki desu*
classical music	クラシック音楽 *kurashikku ongaku*
folk music	フォーク *fooku*
jazz	ジャズ *jazu*
pop music	ポピュラー音楽 *popyuraa ongaku*
rap	ラップ音楽 *rappu ongaku*

If you are looking for popular music and dancing you'll find good quality jazz clubs and conventional discos, even country and- western bars, all in Tokyo's cosmopolitan restaurant districts of Akasaka and Roppongi. Teenagers might like to join in the open-air dancing at Harajuku, near Yoyogi Park.

There are many local and regional festivals throughout the year in Japan. Some examples are; the Snow Festival in Sapporo, from late February to mid-March. In late March to early April the famous Japanese cherry blossoms invite everyone out to enjoy. In May, Kyoto has the Aoi Festival, one of three festivals that reenact Kyoto's history. The other two are the Jidai Festival in October and Gion Festival in July.

Nightlife

What is there to do in the evenings?	夜は何がありますか。*yoru wa nani ga arimasu ka*
Can you recommend…?	いい…はありますか。*ii…wa arimasu ka*
a bar	バー *baa*
a dance club	ディスコ *disuko*
a gay club	ゲイバー *gee baa*
a jazz club	ジャズクラブ *jazu kurabu*
a karaoke bar	カラオケバー *karaoke baa*
a club with Japanese music	日本の音楽が聴けるクラブ *nihon no ongaku ga kikeru kurabu*
Is there live music?	生演奏がありますか。*nama ensoo ga arimasu ka*
How do I get there?	どうやって行くんですか。*dooyatte ikun desu ka*
Is there a cover charge?	カバーチャージはありますか。*kabaa chaaji wa arimasu ka*
Let's go dancing.	ダンスをしに行きましよう。*dansu o shini ikimashoo*
Is this area safe at night?	このあたりは、夜、安全ですか。*kono atari wa yoru anzen desu ka*

YOU MAY HEAR...

携帯電話をお切りください。
keitaidenwa o okiri kudasai

Turn off your cell [mobile] phones, please.

Japan has a wide variety of traditional arts and culture. Some examples from nature are: **bonsai**, an art to recreate nature on a small scale using plants; Japanese gardens, peaceful natural scenes located in cities or temples and **ikebana** or flower arrangement. If you prefer performances, don't miss **bunraku**, puppet theater using dolls of about three feet tall, manipulated by people on the stage. And of course there is **kabuki**, traditional Japanese theater.

Special Requirements

Business Travel

ESSENTIAL

I'm here on business.	仕事で来ました。	*shigoto de kimashita*
Here's my business card.	名刺をどうぞ。	*meeshi o doozo*
Can I have your card?	お名刺をいただけますか。	
	omeeshi o itadakemasu ka	
I have a meeting with...	...さんと会うことになっています。	
	...san to aukoto ni natte imasu	
Where's...?	...はどこですか。 *...wa doko desu ka*	
the business center	ビジネス・センター *bijinesu sentaa*	
the convention hall	会議場 *kaigijoo*	
the meeting room	会議室 *kaigishitsu*	

On Business

I'm here to attend...	...に出るために来ました。	
	...ni derutame ni kimashita	
a seminar	セミナー *seminaa*	
a conference	会議 *kaigi*	
a meeting	会議 *kaigi*	
My name is...	...です。*...desu*	
May I introduce my colleague.	同僚の...をご紹介します。	
	dooryoo no...o goshookai shimasu	
I have a meeting/an appointment with...	...さんとミーティング／約束があります。	
	...san to miitingu/yakusoku ga arimasu	
I'm sorry I'm late.	遅くなって済みません。*osoku natte sumimasen*	
I need an interpreter.	通訳をお願いします。*tsuuyaku o onegai shimasu*	
You can reach me at the...Hotel.	...ホテルに連絡してください。	
	...hoteru ni renraku shite kudasai	
I'm here until...	...までここにいます。*...made kokoni imasu*	

I need to...	...たいんですが。	...tain desu ga
make a call...	電話をかけ	denwa o kake
make a photocopy	コピーをし	kopi o shi
send an e-mail	電子メールを送り	denshimeeru o okuri
send a fax	ファックスを送り	fakkusu o okuri
send a package (overnight)	小包を（翌日配達で）送り	kozutsumi o (yokujitsu haitatsu de) okuri
It was a pleasure to meet you.	お目に掛かれてよかったです。	omenikakarete yokatta desu

For Communications, see page 48.

The exchange of business cards, together with a bow, is the Japanese equivalent of shaking hands, although bowing is not expected of foreign visitors. Visiting cards (**meeshi**) are printed on one side in English and on the other in Japanese. They can be obtained rapidly at most major hotels. Include your occupation or position; if you don't, it will be assumed that your job is of low status.

YOU MAY HEAR...

お約束は承っていますか。	Do you have an
oyakusoku wa uketamawatte imasu ka	appointment?
お会いになりたいのは? *oaini naritai nowa*	With whom?
ただ今会議中でございます。	He/She is in a meeting.
tadaima kaigichuu de gozaimasu	
少々お待ちください。	One moment, please.
shooshoo omachi kudasai	
どうぞお座りください。	Have a seat.
doozo osuwari kudasai	
何かお飲物はいかがですか。	Would you like
nanika onomimono wa ikaga desu ka	something to drink?
お越しいただきましてありがとうござい	Thank you for coming.
ました。*okosi itadakimashite arigatoo*	
gozaimashita	

Traveling with Children

ESSENTIAL

Is there a discount for children?	子供の割引はありますか。
	kodomo no waribiki wa arimasu ka
Can you recommend a baby sitter?	信頼できるベビーシッターを教えてください。
	shinrai dekiru bebii shittaa o oshiete kudasai
Could we have a child's seat/ highchair?	子供用の椅子/ハイチェアをお願いします。
	kodomo yoo no isu/hai chea o onegai shimasu
Where can I change the baby?	おむつはどこで替えられますか。
	omutsu wa doko de kaeraremasu ka

Out & About

Can you recommend something for the kids?	子供が楽しめるところを教えてください。 *kodomo ga tanoshimeru tokoro o oshiete kudasai*
Where's...?	...はどこですか ...*wa doko desu ka*
the amusement park	遊園地 *yuuenchi*
the arcade	ゲームセンター *geemu sentaa*
the kiddie [paddling] pool	子供用のプール *kodomo yoo no puuru*
the playground	公園 *kooen*
the zoo	動物園 *doobutsu en*
Are kids allowed?	子供でも入れますか。*kodomo demo hairemasu ka*
Is it safe for kids?	子供でも大丈夫ですか。 *kodomo demo daijoobu desu ka*
Is it suitable for... year olds?	...歳の子供でも大丈夫ですか。 *...sai no kodomo demo daijoobu desu ka*

Baby Essentials

Do you have...?	...は、ありますか。...*wa arimasu ka*
a baby bottle	哺乳瓶 *honyuubin*
baby wipes	お尻拭き *oshiri fuki*
a car seat	チャイルドシート *chairudo shiito*
a children's menu	お子さまメニュー *okosama menyuu*
a child's seat/ highchair	子供用のイス/ハイチェア *kodomo yoo no isu/haichea*

YOU MAY HEAR...

かわいい！ *kawaii*	How cute!
お名前は？ *onamae wa*	What's his/her name?
何歳ですか。*nansai desu ka*	How old is he/she?

a crib	ベビーベッド *bebii beddo*
diapers [nappies]	(紙)おむつ *(kami) omutsu*
formula	ミルク *miruku*
a pacifier [soother]	おしゃぶり *oshaburi*
a playpen	ベビーサークル *bebii saakuru*
a stroller [pushchair]	ベビーカー *bebiikaa*

| Can I breastfeed the baby here? | ここで授乳してもいいですか。 *kokode junyuu shitemo ii desu ka* |
| Where can I change the baby? | おむつはどこで替えられますか。 *omutsu wa doko de kaeraremasu ka* |

Babysitting

Can you recommend a reliable baby sitter?	信頼できるベビーシッターを教えてください。 *shinrai dekiru bebii shittaa o oshiete kudasai*
What's the charge?	料金 はいくらですか。 *ryookin wa ikura desu ka*
I'll pick them up at…	…に迎えに 行きます。…*ni mukae ni ikimasu*
I can be reached at…	…に電話してください。 …*ni denwa shite Kudasai*

For Time, see page 158.

Health & Emergency

Can you recommend a pediatrician?	小児科医を教えてください。
	shoonikai o oshiete kudasai
My child is allergic to...	うちの子供は…にアレルギーがあります。
	uchi no kodomo wa...ni arerugii ga arimasu
My child is missing.	子供がいなくなりました。
	kodomo ga inaku narimashita
Have you seen a boy/girl?	男/女の子を見ましたか。
	otoko/onna no ko o mimashita ka

Disabled Travelers

ESSENTIAL

Is there...?	…はありますか。*...wa arimasu ka*
access for the disabled	身体障害者用通路 *shintai shogaisha yoo tsuuro*
a wheelchair ramp	車椅子用スロープ *kuruma isu yoo suroopu*
a handicapped [disabled] accessible toilet	ハンディキャップ用トイレ *handikyappu yoo toire*
I need...	… が要るんですが。*...ga irun desu ga*
assistance	助け *tasuke*
an elevator [lift]	エレベーター *erebeetaa*
a ground floor room	1階の部屋 *ikkai no heya*

Many provincial main stations have elevators and other facilities for disabled travelers. However, smaller stations generally do not.

Asking for Assistance

I'm disabled.	私は身体が不自由です。
	watashi wa karada ga fujiyuu desu
I'm deaf.	私は耳が聞こえません。
	watashi wa mimi ga kikoemasen
I'm visually/hearing impaired.	私は目がよく見えません／耳がよく聞こえません。
	watashi wa me ga yoku miemasen/mimi ga yoku kikoemasen
I'm unable to walk far/use the stairs.	私は遠くまで歩けません／階段を上れません。
	watashi wa tooku made arukemasen/kaidan o noboremasen
Can I bring my wheelchair?	車椅子を持っていってもいいですか。
	kurumaisu o motte ittemo ii desu ka
Are guide dogs permitted?	盲導犬が入ってもいいですか。
	moodooken ga haittemo ii desu ka
Can you help me?	助けてください。*tasukete kudasai*
Please open/hold the door.	ドアを開けて／開けておいてください。
	doa o akete/akete oite kudasai

In an Emergency

Emergencies

ESSENTIAL

Help!	助けて!	*tasukete*
Go away!	あっちへ行け!	*atchi e ike*
Call the police!	警察を呼んで!	*keesatsu o yonde*
Stop thief!	泥棒!	*doroboo*
Get a doctor!	医者を呼んで!	*isha o yonde*
Fire!	火事だ!	*kaji da*
I'm lost.	道に迷いました。	*michi ni mayoimashita*
Can you help me?	助けてください。	*tasukete kudasai*

In an emergency, dial: **110** for the police;
119 for the fire brigade and emergency medical services.

YOU MAY HEAR...

この用紙に記入してください。	Please fill out this form.
kono yooshi ni kinyuu shite kudasai	
身分証明書を見せてください。	Your identification, please.
mibun shoomeisho o misete kudasai	
いつ／どこで起きたんですか。	When/Where did it happen?
itsu/dokode okitan desu ka	
どんな顔をしていますか。	What does he/she look like?
donna kao o shite iamsu ka	

Police

ESSENTIAL

Call the police!	警察を呼んで! *keesatsu o yonde*
Where's the police station?	交番はどこですか。*kooban wa doko desu ka*
There has been an accident/attack.	事故がありました／襲われました。 *jiko ga arimashita/osowaremashita*
My child is missing.	子供がいなくなりました。 *kodomo ga inaku narimashita*
I need an interpreter.	通訳が要るんですが。*tsuuyaku ga irun desu ga*
I need...	…したいんですが。*...shitain desu ga*
to contact my lawyer	弁護士に連絡 *bengoshi ni renraku*
to make a phonecall	電話 *denwa*
I'm innocent.	無実です。*mujitsu desu*

Crime & Lost Property

I want to report...	…を報告したいんですが。 *...o hookoku shitaindesu ga*
a mugging	強盗 *gootoo*
a rape	レイプ *reepu*
a theft	泥棒 *doroboo*
I've been mugged.	強盗にあいました。*gootoo ni aimashita*
I've lost my...	…をなくしました。*...o nakushimashita*
My...has been stolen	…を盗まれました。*...o nusumaremashita*
backpack	リュックサック *ryukkusakku*
bicycle	自転車 *jitensha*
camera	カメラ *kamera*

car	車 *kuruma*
rental car	レンタカー *renta kaa*
computer	コンピュータ *konpyuuta*
credit cards	クレジットカード *kurejitto kaado*
jewelry	宝石 *hooseki*
money	お金 *okane*
passport	パスポート *pasupooto*
purse/wallet	財布 *saifu*
traveler's checks [cheques]	トラベラーズチェック *toraberaazu chekku*

I need a police report for my insurance claim.	保険の申請に警察の証明書が要ります。 *hoken no shinsee ni keesatsu no shoomeesho ga irimasu*
Where is the British/American/Irish embassy?	英国/アメリカ/アイルランド大使館はどこですか。*eikoku / amerika / airurando taishikan wa doko desu ka*
I need an interpreter.	通訳が必要です。*tsuuyaku ga hitsuyoo desu*

Health

ESSENTIAL

I'm sick.	具合が悪いんです。*guai ga waruin desu*
I need an English-speaking doctor.	英語ができる医者はいますか。*eego ga dekiru isha wa imasu ka*
It hurts here.	ここが痛いんです。*koko ga itain desu*
I have a stomachache.	お腹が痛いんです。*onaka ga itain desu*

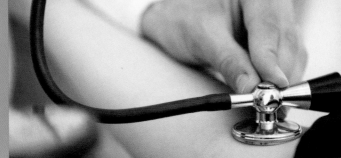

Finding a Doctor

Can you recommend a doctor/dentist?	医者/歯医者を教えてください。 *isha/haisha o oshiete kudasai*
Could the doctor come to see me here?	往診してくれますか。 *ooshin shite kuremasu ka*
I need an English-speaking doctor.	英語ができる医者はいますか。 *eego ga dekiru isha wa imasu ka*
What are the office hours?	診察時間はいつですか。 *shinsatsu jikan wa itsu desu ka*
Can I make an appointment...?	...予約したいんですが。 *...yoyaku shitain desu ga*
for today	今日 *kyoo*
for tomorrow	明日 *ashita*
as soon as possible	できるだけ早く *dekirudake hayaku*
It's urgent.	至急お願いします。 *shikyuu onegai shimasu*

Symptoms

I'm...	しています。 *shite imasu*
bleeding	出血 *shukketsu*
constipated	便秘 *benpi*
dizzy	目眩 *memai*
It hurts here.	ここが痛いんです。 *koko ga itai n desu*

I'm nauseous/ 吐きそうです/吐いています。
vomiting. *hakisoo desu/haite imasu*

I have... ...があります。*...ga arimasu*

- an allergic reaction アレルギー反応 *arerugii hannoo*
- chest pain 胸の痛み *mune no itami*
- an earache 耳の痛み *mimi no itami*
- a fever 熱 *netsu*
- pain 痛み *itami*
- a rash 発疹 *hasshin*
- some swelling 腫れ *hare*

I have a sprain. ねんざしました。*nenza shimashita*

I have a stomachache. お腹が痛いんです。*onaka ga itain desu*

I have sunstroke. 日射病にかかりました。
nisshabyoo ni kakarimashita

I've been sick for...days...日間, 病気です。*...nichikan byooki desu*

YOU MAY HEAR...

どうしましたか。*doo shimashita ka* — What's wrong?

どこが痛みますか。*doko ga itamimasu ka* — Where does it hurt?

ここが痛みますか。*koko ga itamimasu ka* — Does it hurt here?

他に薬を飲んでいますか。
hokani kusuri o nonde imasu ka — Are you taking any other medication?

何かのアレルギーはありますか。
nanka no arerugii wa arimasu ka — Are you allergic to anything?

口を開けてください。*kuchi o akete kudasai* — Open your mouth.

深呼吸してください。
shin kokyuu shite kudasai — Breathe deeply.

病院に行ってください。
byooin ni itte kudasai — Please go to the hospital.

Conditions

I'm.	...です。 ...desu
anemic	貧血症 hinketsu shoo
asthmatic	ぜんそく zensoku
diabetic	糖尿病 toonyoo byoo
epileptic	てんかん症 tenkanshoo
I'm allergic to antibiotics/penicillin.	抗生物質／ペニシリンにアレルギーがあります。 koosei busshitsu/penishirin ni arerugii ga arimasu
I have arthritis.	関節炎にかかっています。 kansetsuen ni kakatte imasu
I have (high/low) blood pressure.	高／低血圧です。koo/tei ketsuatsu desu
I have a heart condition.	心臓が悪いんです。shinzoo ga waruin desu
I'm on...	...を飲んでいます。 ...o nonde imasu
I'm ...months pregnant	妊娠 ...ヶ月です。ninshin ... ka getsu desu

Treatment

Do I need a prescription /medicine?	処方箋/薬が必要ですか。 shohoo sen / kusuri ga hitsuyoo desu ka
Can you prescribe a generic drug [unbranded medication]?	後発医薬品を処方してもらえますか。 koohatsu iyakuhin o shohoo shite morae masu ka
Where can I get it?	どこで買えますか。doko de kae masu ka

For What to Take, see page 149.

Hospital

Please notify my family.	家族に知らせてください。 kazoku ni shirasete kudasai

I'm in pain.	痛みます。*itamimasu*
I need a doctor/nurse.	医者／看護師を呼んでください。
	isha/kangoshi o yonde kudasai
When are visiting hours?	面会時間はいつですか。
	menkai jikan wa itsu desu ka
I'm visiting.	…の見舞いに来ました。*…no mimai ni kimashita*

Dentist

I've broken a tooth/lost a filling.	歯を折りました／詰め物をなくしました。
	ha o orimashita/tsumemono o nakushimashita
I have a toothache.	歯が痛いんです。*ha ga itain desu*
Can you fix this denture?	この入れ歯を直せますか。
	kono ireba o naosemasu ka

Gynecologist

I have menstrual cramps/a vaginal infection.	生理痛／膣感染症があります。
	seeritsuu/chitsu kansen shoo ga arimasu
I missed my period	生理がありませんでした。
	seeri ga arimasen deshita
I'm on the Pill.	ピルを飲んでいます。*piru o nonde imasu*

I'm pregnant/not pregnant.	妊娠しています/いません。
	ninshin shite imasu/imasen
I haven't had my period for...months.	生理が…ヶ月間ありません。
	seeri ga... kagetsukan arimasen

Optician

I've lost.	…をなくしました。 *...o nakushimashita*
one of my contact lenses	片方のコンタクトレンズ
	katahoo no kontakuto renzu
my glasses	眼鏡 *megane*
a lens	レンズ *renzu*

Payment & Insurance

How much?	いくらですか。 *ikura desuka*
Can I pay by credit card?	クレジットカードを使えますか。
	kurejitto kaado o tsukaemasu ka
I have insurance.	保険に入っています。 *hoken ni haitte imasu*
Can I have a receipt for my insurance?	保険申請のためにレシートをください。
	hoken shinsee no tame ni reshiito o kudasai

Pharmacy

ESSENTIAL

Where's the nearest (all-night) pharmacy?	（夜間営業の）薬局はどこですか。
	(yakan eegyoo no) yakkyoku wa doko desu ka
What time does the pharmacy open/close?	薬局は何時に開き/閉まりますか。
	yakkyoku wa nanji ni aki/shimari masu ka
What would you recommend for...?	…には何がいいですか。
	...niwa nani ga ii desu ka

How much should I take?	どのくらい飲むんですか。
	dono kurai nomun desu ka
Can you fill [makeup] this prescription for me?	この薬をください。 *kono kusuri o kudasai*
I'm allergic to...	私は…にアレルギーがあります。
	watashi wa… ni arerugii ga arimasu

You will find a large selection of imported medications at the American Pharmacy in Tokyo. These can be more expensive than at home, so if you have any special medical needs it is best to bring an ample supply with you.

What to Take

How much should I take?	どのくらい飲むんですか。
	dono kurai nomun desu ka
How many times a day should I take it?	一日何回飲むんですか。 *ichinichi nankai nomun desu ka*
Is it suitable for children?	子供でも飲めますか。 *kodomo demo nomemasu ka*
I'm taking...	…を飲んでいます。 *…o nonde imasu*
Are there side effects?	副作用はありますか。 *fukusayoo wa arimasu ka*
I'd like some medicine for...	…の薬をください。 *…no kusuri o kudasai*
a cold	風邪 *kaze*
a cough	咳 *seki*
diarrhea	下痢 *geri*
a headache	頭痛 *zutsuu*
a toothache	歯が痛い *haga itai*

YOU MAY SEE...

一日一回／三回	once/three times a day
錠	tablet(s)
滴	drop
ティースプーン／茶さじ	teaspoon(s)
食前／食後／食間	before/after/in between meals
空腹時	on an empty stomach
丸ごと飲み下し	swallow whole
眠気を催すことがあります	may cause drowsiness
外用薬	for external use only

I'd like some medicine for...	…の薬をください。 *…no kusuri o kudasai*
insect bites	虫刺され *mushi sasare*
motion [travel] sickness	乗物酔い *norimono yoi*
a sore throat	喉の痛み *nodo no itami*
sunburn	日焼け *hiyake*
an upset stomach	胃痛 *itsuu*

Basic Supplies

I'd like...	…が欲しいんですが 。 *…ga hoshiin desu ga*
acetaminophen [paracetamol]	アセタミノーフェン *asetaminoofen*
antiseptic cream	傷薬 *kizugusuri*
aspirin	頭痛薬 *zutsuuyaku*
bandages	包帯 *hootai*
a comb	櫛 *kushi*
condoms	コンドーム *kondoomu*
contact lens solution	コンタクトレンズ液 *kontakutorenzu eki*

deodorant	デオドラント *deodoranto*
a hairbrush	ヘアブラシ *heaburashi*
hair spray	ヘアスプレー *hea supuree*
ibuprofen	イブプロフェン *ibupuroren*
insect repellent	防虫剤 *boochuuzai*
a nail file	ネイルファイル *neirufairu*
a (disposable) razor	(使い捨て) カミソリ *(tsukaisuite) kamisori*
razor blades	カミソリの刃 *kamisori no ha*
sanitary napkins [pads]	生理用ナプキン *seeri yoo napukin*
shampoo/ conditioner	シャンプー/コンディショナー *shanpuu/kondishonaa*
soap	石鹸 *sekken*
sunscreen	日焼け止めクリーム *hiyake dome kuriimu*
tampons	タンポン *tanpon*
tissues	ティッシュペーパー *tisshu peepaa*
toilet paper	トイレットペーパー *toiretto peepaa*
toothpaste	歯磨き粉 *hamigakiko*

For Baby Essentials, see page 136.

For Meals & Cooking, see page 64.

The Basics

Grammar

Regular Verbs

At first glance Japanese verbs are very straightforward, with only present and past tenses and no special form to indicate person or number. Future tense is gauged from the context.

However, verbs are subject to other changes to express variety of degrees of politeness and mood. The two basic verb forms are:

taberu	to eat		**nomu**	to drink
tabemasu	to eat		**nomimasu**	to drink
(polite form)			(polite form)	

This phrase book uses the polite form throughout.

tabemasu	(I, you, he, she, we, they) eat
tabemasen	(I, you, he, she, we, they) don't/doesn't eat
tabemashita	(I, you, he, she, we, they) ate
tabemasendeshita	(I, you, he, she, we, they) didn't eat

In addition to the above forms, verbs can indicate such functions as causative, command, conditional, passive, potential etc. by adding appropriate suffixes. For example:

tabesasemasu	I cause (someone) to eat
tabero!	Eat!
tabereba	if you eat...

Particles

Japanese uses a number of particles to mark the use, or add to the meaning of the word they follow in a sentence.

ga	subject marker	**nodo ga itai desu**	literal meaning: The throat is sore.
wa	attention-directing marker	**watashi wa nodo ga itai desu**	literal meaning: As for me the throat is sore.

| **o** | object marker | **gohan o tabemasu** | literal meaning: I eat rice. |

Irregular Verbs

Japanese has only two irregular verbs: **suru** (to do) and **kuru** (to come). Their polite forms are as follows:

shimasu	do	**kimasu**	come
shimasen	don't/ doesn't do	**kimasen**	don't/ doesn't come
shimashita	did	**kimashita**	came
shimasendeshita	didn't do	**kimasendeshita**	didn't come

Nouns & Articles

Japanese nouns have no articles, and no plurals. All nouns have one single form that does not change according to the noun's role in a sentence. Personal pronouns are used sparingly in Japanese. Use the person's name + **san** instead of a pronoun, or omit the pronoun completely if it is clear who is being addressed or referred to. Personal pronouns are:

watashib	I	**anata*** (singular)	you
watashi tachi	we	**anatagata*** (plural)	you

* These pronouns are very familiar and appropriate only between husband and wife or boyfriend and girlfriend.

Word Order

Japanese questions are formed by adding the particle **ka** (a verbal question mark) to the verb at the end of a sentence. Note that in Japanese the verb always comes last. The basic rule for word order within a sentence is: subject - object - verb

Watashi wa Smith desu.	I'm (Mr./Mrs.) Smith.
Honda-san* desu ka?	Are you (Mr./Mrs.) Honda?

*When addressing a Japanese person you should use the family name followed by san. (Do not use san when referring to yourself!)

Imperatives

There are many ways to indicate an order, depending on how strong you would like it to be. Following is an example of imperative from mild to strong:

Go! **Itte**   **Ikinasai**   **Ike**

Comparative & Superlative

Unlike English, Japanese adjectives do not indicate comparative or superlative. Instead Japanese employs the following pattern:

Comparative: A **to** B **to dochira ga** adjective **desuka?**

Tookyoo to Oosaka to dochira ga ookii desu ka.

Which is bigger, Tokyo or Osaka?

Superlative: **A to** B **to** C **de A ga ichiban** adjective **desu**.

Tookyoo to Oosaka to Kyooto de Tookyoo ga ichiban ookii desu.

Among Tokyo, Osaka and Kyoto, Tokyo is the biggest.

Possessive Pronouns

To make possessive pronouns, use the grammar marker **no** following the person's name or the personal pronoun.

Honda-san no hon   Mr./Mrs. Honda's book
Watashi no hon   my book

Adjectives

A Japanese adjective ends in **i** and modifies a noun that is placed immediately after it. For example, 'a big room' will be **ookii heya**. Japanese adjectives are very different from their English counter parts, and behave more like verbs. The past tense of most adjectives is formed by adding **-katta** to the basic stem:

takai   expensive   **yasui**   cheap
takakatta   (was) expensive   **yasukatta**   (was)cheap

There is another group of adjectives that takes **na** at the end of the word to modify a noun.

Example: **kiree-na hana** (pretty flower), **taisetsu-na mono** (an important thing), **shizuka-na tokoro** (a quiet place).

Adverbs

An adverb describes a verb. Many Japanese adverbs end in **ku**, and are derived from adjectives by replacing the final **i** of an adjective with **ku**.

Example: **Hayaku hashirimashita. He ran quickly.**

Numbers

ESSENTIAL

0	零/ゼロ *ree/zero*
1	一 *ichi*
2	二 *ni*
3	三 *san*
4	四 *shi/yon*
5	五 *go*
6	六 *roku*
7	七 *shichi/nana*
8	八 *hachi*
9	九 *kyuu/ku*
10	十 *juu*
11	十一 *juuichi*
12	十二 *juuni*
13	十三 *juusan*
14	十四 *juushi/juuyon*
15	十五 *juugo*
16	十六 *juuroku*
17	十七 *juushichi/juunana*
18	十八 *juuhachi*
19	十九 *juukyuu/juuku*
20	二十 *nijuu*
21	二十一 *nijuuichi*
22	二十二 *nijuuni*

30	三十 *sanjuu*
31	三十一 *sanjuuichi*
40	四十 *yonjuu/shijuu*
50	五十 *gojuu*
60	六十 *rokujuu*
70	七十 *nanajuu/shichijuu*
80	八十 *hachijuu*
90	九十 *kyuujuu*
100	百 *hyaku*
101	百一 *hyakuichi*
200	二百 *nihyaku*
500	五百 *gohyaku*
1,000	千 *sen*
10,000	一万 *ichiman*
1,000,000	百万 *hyakuman*

Ordinal Numbers

first	一番 *ichiban*
second	二番 *niban*
third	三番 *sanban*
fourth	四番 *yonban*
fifth	五番 *goban*
once	一回 *ikkai*
twice	二回 *nikai*
three times	三回 *sankai*

In Japanese, there are two ways of counting to ten. There are general numbers (listed on page 155) used for talking about sums of money, telephone numbers, etc. There is also a system for combining a number with an object-specific counter. This system groups objects into types according to shape and size. There are specific ways of counting flat objects, animals, people, etc. Luckily the counter system only applies to numbers from 1-10. After 10 the general number is used. When you are not sure of the correct counter, you can always use the 'all-purpose' counters listed below.

'All-purpose' Counters (Numbers 1 - 10)

These counters are strictly used to count 'unclassifiable' objects (objects where shape or size are difficult to determine). When you don't know the specific counter use:

1	**hitotsu**	2	**futatsu**
3	**mittsu**	4	**yottsu**
5	**itsutsu**	6	**muttsu**
7	**nanatsu**	8	**yattsu**
9	**kokonotsu**	10	**too**

Other Counters

Flat objects (stamps, paper, etc.)

1	**ichimai**	6	**rokumai**
2	**nimai**	7	**nanamai/shichimai**
3	**sanmai**	8	**hachimai**
4	**yonmai**	9	**kyuumai**
5	**gomai**	10	**juumai**

People

1	**hitori**	6	**rokunin**
2	**futari**	7	**nananin/shichinin**
3	**sannin**	8	**hachinin**
4	**yonin**	9	**kyuunin**
5	**gonin**	10	**juunin**

Long, thin objects (pen, bottle, umbrella, etc.)

1	**ippon**	6	**roppon**
2	**nihon**	7	**nanahon**
3	**sanbon**	8	**happon**
4	**yonhon**	9	**kyuuhon**
5	**gohon**	10	**juppon**

For example, the counter for a bottle is **nihon**.

I'd like two bottles of beer.　　　**Biru o nihon kudasai.**

If you didn't know the counter, you could use the 'all-purpose' counter:

I'd like two bottles of beer.　　　**Biiru o futatsu kudasai.**

Note that the counter usually follows the word it qualifies.

Time

ESSENTIAL

What time is it?	何時ですか。 *nanji desu ka*
It's noon [midday].	十二時 (正午) です。 *juuniji (shoogo) desu*
At midnight.	真夜中に *mayonaka ni*
From nine o'clock to 5 o'clock.	九時から五時まで *kuji kara goji made*
Twenty [after] past four	四時二十分 *yoji nijuppun*
A quarter to nine	九時十五分前 *kuji juugorun mae*
5:30 a.m./p.m.	午前/午後五時三十分 *gozen/gogo goji sanjuppun*

In ordinary conversation, time is expressed as shown above. For airline and train timetables, however, the 24-hour clock is used. Japan is nine hours ahead of GMT all year round. Japan does not change its clocks to reflect winter and summer time.

Days

ESSENTIAL

Sunday	日曜日	*nichiyoobi*
Monday	月曜日	*getsuyoobi*
Tuesday	火曜日	*kayoobi*
Wednesday	水曜日	*suiyoobi*
Thursday	木曜日	*mokuyoobi*
Friday	金曜日	*kinyoobi*
Saturday	土曜日	*doyoobi*

Dates

yesterday	昨日	*kinoo*
today	今日	*kyoo*
tomorrow	明日	*ashita*
day	日	*nichi/hi*

Japan changed from lunar calendar to the Gregorian calendar in 1873. However, the lunar calendar is still used in farming, and in other activities in rural areas of Japan. Japanese calendars start with Sunday and end with Saturday.

Dates in Japan are written in Year-Month-Day format. January 1st, 2010 would be 2010 年1月1日 **nisen juu nen ichi gatsu tsuitachi**, or 2010, January, first.

week	週 *shuu*
month	月 *tsuki*
year	年 *toshi*

Months

January	一月 *ichigatsu*
February	二月 *nigatsu*
March	三月 *sangatsu*
April	四月 *shigatsu*
May	五月 *gogatsu*
June	六月 *rokugatsu*
July	七月 *shichigatsu*

The most important holiday in Japan is New Year's day. All the stores are closed on the January first, and some will close on the second and third as well. Adult's Day (second Monday in January) is designated to celebrate those who are and will be 20 during the year. The week from Greenery Day (April 29) to Children's Day (May 5) is called the Golden Week. Many people take advantage of the four holidays falling during this week (Greenery Day, May Day, Constitution Day, and Children's Day) to travel, thus creating traffic jams everywhere. Bon Festival, from August 13 to 16, is a time when many people go to their ancestral home: the souls of the deceased ancestors are considered to come home during this time.

August	ノ月 *hachigatsu*
September	九月 *kugatsu*
October	十月 *juugatsu*
November	十一月 *juuichigatsu*
December	十二月 *juunigatsu*

Seasons

the spring	春 *haru*
the summer	夏 *natsu*
the fall [autumn]	秋 *aki*
the winter	冬 *fuyu*

Holidays

Public holidays

January 1 ganjitsu/gantan New Year's Day

Second Monday in January seejin no hi Adult's Day

February 11 kenkoku kinen no hi National Foundation Day

March 21* shunbun no hi Vernal Equinox Day

April 29 midori no hi Greenery Day

May 3 kenpoo kinen bi Constitution Day

May 5 kodomo no hi Children's Day

September 15 keeroo no hi Respect for the Aged Day

September 23* shuubun no hi Autumnal Equinox Day

October 10 taiiku no hi Health-Sports Day

November 3 bunka no hi Culture Day

November 23 kinroo kansha no hi Labor Thanksgiving Day

December 23 tennoo tanjoobi Emperor's Birthday

* These dates are lunar and change year by year.

Conversion Tables

Mileage

1 km – 0.62 mi	20 km – 12.4 mi
5 km – 3.10 mi	50 km – 31.0 mi
10 km – 6.20 mi	100 km – 61.0 mi

Measurement

1 gram	グラム *guramu*	=1000 milligrams	=0.035 oz.
1 kilogram (kg)	キログラム *kiroguramu*	=1000 grams	=2.2 lb
1 liter (l)	リットル *rittoru*	=1000 milliliters	=1.06 U.S./0.88 Brit. quarts
1 centimeter (cm)	センチ *senta*	=10 millimeters	=0.4 inch
1 meter (m)	メートル *meetoru*	=100 centimeters	=39.37 inches/ 3.28 feet
1 kilometer (km)	キロメートル *kiromeetoru*	=1000 meters	=0.62 mile

Temperature

-40°C – -40°F	1°C – 30°F	20°C – 68°F
-30°C – -22°F	0°C – 32°F	25°C – 77°F
-20°C – -4°F	5°C – 41°F	30°C – 86°F
-10°C – 14°F	10°C – 50°F	35°C – 95°F
-5°C – 23°F	15°C – 59°F	

Oven Temperature

100°C – 212°F	177°C – 350°F
121°C – 250°F	204°C – 400°F
149°C – 300°F	204°C – 400°F

Dictionary

English–Japanese

A

a.m. 午前 gozen

abbey 修道院 shuudooin

access v (Internet) アクセスします akusesu shimasu

accident 事故 jiko

accommodation 宿泊設備 shukuhaku setsubi

account n 会計 kaikee

acupuncture 鍼 hari

adapter アダプタ adaputa

address 住所 juusho

after …の後 …no ato

afternoon 午後 gogo

aftershave アフターシェーブ afutaa sheebu

age 年齢 nenree

agency 代理店 dairiten

AIDS エイズ eezu

air conditioning エアコン eakon

air pump エアポンプ eaponpu

airline 航空会社 kookuu gaisha

airmail 航空便 kookuubin

airplane 飛行機 hikooki

airport 空港 kuukoo

aisle 通路 tsuuro

aisle seat 通路側の座席 tsuurogawa no zaseki

allergic アレルギー arerugii

allergic reaction アレルギー反応 arerugii hannoo

alone 一人の人 hitori no hito

alter v (clothing) 直します naoshi masu

alternate route 他の道 hoka no michi

aluminum foil アルミホイル arumi hoiru

amazing すごい sugoi

ambulance 救急車 kyuukyuusha

American アメリカの amerika no

amusement park 遊園地 yuuenchi

anemic 貧血の hinketsu no

anesthesia 麻酔 masui

animal 動物 doobutsu

ankle 足首 ashikubi

antibiotic 抗生物質 koosee busshitsu

antiques store 骨董店 kottooten

antiseptic cream 傷薬 kizugusuri

anything 何でも nandemo

| **adj** adjective | **BE** British English | **prep** preposition |
| **adv** adverb | **n** noun | **v** verb |

apartment マンション manshon

appendix (body part) 盲腸 moochoo

appetizer おつまみ otsumami

appointment 予約 yoyaku

arcade アーケード aakeedo

area code 市外局番 shigai kyokuban

arm 腕 ude

aromatherapy アロマセラピー aroma serapii

around (the corner) 道を曲がった ところ michi o magatta tokoro

arrivals (airport) 到着 toochaku

arrive v 着きます tsuki masu

artery 動脈 doomyaku

arthritis 関節炎 kansetsuen

Asian アジアの ajia no

aspirin 頭痛薬 zutsuuyaku

asthmatic 喘息の zensoku no

ATM キャッシュコーナー kyasshu koonaa

attack v 襲います osoimasu

attend v 出席します shusseki shimasu

attraction (place) アトラクション atorakushon

attractive 魅力的 miryokuteki

Australian オーストラリア人 oosutorariajin

automatic 自動 jidoo

automatic car オートマチック ootomachikku

B

baby 赤ちゃん akachan

baby bottle 哺乳瓶 honyuubin

baby wipe おしりふき oshirifuki

babysitter ベビーシッター bebii shittaa

back (body part) 背中 senaka

backpack リュックサック ryukkusakku

bag バッグ baggu

baggage [BE] 荷物 nimotsu

baggage claim 荷物引渡所 nimotsu hikiwatashijo

baggage ticket 荷物引換証 nimotsu hikikaeshoo

bakery パン屋 pan-ya

ballet バレエ baree

bandage 包帯 hootai

bank 銀行 ginkoo

bar バー baa

barber 床屋 tokoya

baseball 野球 yakyuu

basket (grocery store) かご kago

basketball バスケットボール basuketto booru

bathroom 風呂場 furoba

bathroom (toilet) トイレ toire

battery 電池 denchi

battleground 戦場跡 senjooato

beach 海岸／ビーチ kaigan/biichi

beautiful 美しい utsukushii

bed ベッド beddo

begin v 始めます hajime masu

before 前 mae

beginner 初心者 shoshinsha

behind 後ろ ushiro

beige ベージュ beeju

belt ベルト beruto

berth 寝台 shindai

best 一番いい ichiban ii

better もっといい motto ii

bicycle 自転車 jitensha

big 大きい ookii

bigger もっと大きい motto ookii

bike route 自転車ルート jitensha ruuto

bikini ビキニ bikini

bill v (charge) 請求します seekyuu shimasu; ~ n (money) 紙幣 shihee; ~ n (of sale) 請求書 seekyuusho; **itemized** ~ 明細書 meesaisho

bird 鳥 tori

birthday 誕生日 tanjoobi

black 黒い kuroi

bladder 膀胱 bookoo

bland 味が薄い aji ga usui

blanket 毛布 moofu

bleed v 出血します shukketsu shimasu

blood 血液 ketsueki

blood pressure 血圧 ketsuatsu

blouse ブラウス burausu

blue ブルー buruu

board v (plane) 搭乗します toojoo shimasu, (train) 乗車します joosha shimasu

boarding pass 搭乗券 toojoo ken

boat ボート booto

bone 骨 hone

book 本 hon

bookstore 本屋 hon-ya

boots ブーツ buutu

boring つまらない tsumaranai

botanical garden 植物園 shokubut-suen

bother v 邪魔します jama shimasu

bottle 瓶 bin

bottle opener 栓抜き sennuki

bowl ボール booru

box 箱 hako

boy 男の子 otoko noko

boyfriend ボーイフレンド booi furendo

bra ブラジャー burajaa

bracelet ブレスレット buresuretto

brakes (car) ブレーキ bureeki

break v 折れます oremasu

break-in (burglary) 侵入します shinnyuu shimasu

breakdown 故障 koshoo

breakfast 朝食 chooshoku

breast 乳房 chibusa

breastfeed 母乳をあげます bonyuu o agemasu

breathe v 呼吸します kokyuu shimasu

bridge 橋 hashi

briefs (clothing) ブリーフ buriifu

bring (people) v 連れてきます tsurete kimasu; **(things)** 持ってきます motte kimasu

British イギリス人 igirisujin

broken 壊れた kowareta

brooch ブローチ buroochi

broom 箒 hooki

brother (my older) 兄 ani

brother (my younger) 弟 otooto

brother (someone else's older) お兄さん oniisan

brother (someone else's younger) 弟さん otootosan

brown 茶色 chairo

bug 虫 mushi

building ビル/建物 biru/tatemono

burn v 焼きます yakimasu

bus バス basu

bus station バスターミナル basu taaminaru

bus stop バス停留所/バス停 basu teeryuujo/basutee

bus ticket バスの切符 basu no kippu

bus tour バス旅行 basu ryokoo

business 仕事 shigoto

business card 名刺 meeshi

business center ビジネス・センター bijinesu sentaa

business class ビジネス・クラス bijinesu kurasu

business hours 営業時間 eegyoo jikan

butcher 肉屋 nikuya

buttocks お尻 oshiri

buy v 買います kaimasu

bye ごめんください gomen kudasai

C

cabin キャビン kyabin

cable car ケーブル・カー keeburu kaa

café 喫茶店 kissaten

call v 電話します denwa shimasu

calligraphy supplies 習字用具 shuuji yoogu

calories カロリー karorii

camera カメラ kamera

camp v キャンプします kyanpu shimasu; **no ~ing** キャンプ禁止 kyanpu kinshi

campsite キャンプ場 kyanpujoo

can opener 缶切り kankiri

Canada カナダ kanada

Canadian カナダ人 kanadajin

cancel v キャンセルします kyanseru shimasu

candy キャンデー kyandee

canned good 缶詰 kanzume

canyon 峡谷 kyookoku

car 車 kuruma

car hire [BE] レンタカー rentakaa

car park [BE] 駐車場 chuushajoo

car rental レンタカー rentakaa

car seat チャイルドシート chairudo shiito

carafe カラフ karafu

card カード kaado

carry-on 手荷物 tenimotsu

cart カート kaato

carton カートン kaaton

case (amount) ケース keesu

cash v 換金します kankin shimasu; ~ n 現金 genkin

cash advance キャッシング・サービス kyasshingu saabisu

cashier 会計 kaikee

casino カジノ kajino

castle お城 oshiro

cathedral 大聖堂 daiseedoo

cave 洞窟 dookutsu

CD CD shii dii

cell phone 携帯電話 keetai denwa

Celsius 接氏 sesshi

centimeter センチメートル senchi

-meetoru

chair 椅子 isu

chair lift スキーリフト sukii rifuto

change v **(buses)** 乗り換えます norikaemasu; ~ v **(money)** 替えます kaemasu; ~ v **(baby)** おむつを替えます omutsu o kaemasu; ~ n **(plan)** 変更 henkoo; ~ n **(money)** お釣り otsuri

charcoal 炭 sumi

charge v **(credit card)** カードで払います kaado de haraimasu; n **(cost)** 料金 ryookin

cheap 安い yasui

cheaper もっと安い motto yasui

check v **(something)** 調べます shirabemasu; ~ v **(luggage)** 預けます azukemasu; ~ n **(payment)** お勘定 okanjoo

check-in チェックイン chekku in

checking account 当座預金口座 tooza yoking kooza

check-out (hotel) n チェックアウト chekku auto

chemical toilet ケミカルトイレ kemikaru toire

chemist [BE] 薬局 yakkyoku

cheque [BE] チェック chekku

chest (body part) 胸 mune

chest pain 胸の痛み mune no itami

chewing gum ガム gamu

child 子供 kodomo

child's seat 子供用の椅子 kodomoyoo no isu

children's menu 子供用の メニュー kodomoyoo no menyuu

children's portion 子供用の メニュー kodomoyoo no menyuu

china 瀬戸物 setomono

China 中国 chuugoku

Chinese (language) 中国語 chuugokugo

Chinese (people) 中国人 chuugokujin

chopsticks おはし ohashi

church 教会 kyookai

cigar 葉巻 hamaki

cigarette 煙草 tabako

class クラス kurasu

clay pot 土器 doki

classical music クラシック音楽 kurashikku ongaku

clean v きれいにします kirei ni shimasu; ~ adj きれい kiree

cleaning product 洗浄剤 senjoozai

cleaning supplies クリーニング用 品 kuriiningu yoohin

clear v (on an ATM) 消去します shookyo shimasu

cliff 崖 gake

cling film [BE] ラップ rappu

close v (a shop) 閉めます shimemasu; ~ adj 近い chikai

closed 閉館 heekan

clothing 衣類 irui

clothing store 洋服屋 yoofukuya

club クラブ kurabu

coat コート kooto

coffee shop 喫茶店 kissaten

coin 硬貨 kooka

cold (sickness) 風邪 kaze; ~ (weather) 寒い samui; ~ (food) 冷たい tsumetai

colleague 同僚 dooryoo

cologne オーデコロン oodekoron

color 色 iro

comb 櫛 kushi

come v 来ます kimasu

complaint 苦情 kujoo

computer コンピュータ konpyuuta

concert コンサート konsaato

concert hall コンサートホール konsaato hooru

condition (medical) 症状 shoojoo

conditioner コンディショナー kondishonaa

condom コンドーム kondoomu

conference 会議 kaigi

confirm v 確認します kakunin shimasu

congestion 混雑 konzatsu

connect v (internet) 接続します setsuzoku shimasu

connection (internet) 接続 setsuzoku; **~ (flight)** 連絡 renraku

constipated 便秘 benpi

consulate 領事館 ryoojikan

consultant コンサルタント konsarutanto

contact v 連絡します renraku shimasu

contact lens コンタクトレンズ kontakuto renzu; **~ solution** コンタクトレンズ液 kontakuto renzu eki

contagious 伝染性 densensee

convention hall 会議場 kaigijoo

conveyor belt コンベヤーベルト konbeyaa beruto

cook v 料理します ryoori shimasu

cooking gas ガス gasu

cool (temperature) 涼しい suzushii

copper 銅 doo

corkscrew コルクスクリュー koruku sukuryuu

cost v かかります kakarimasu

cot 折り畳みベッド oritatami beddo

cotton 綿／コットン men/kotton

cough 咳 seki

country code 国番号 kuni bangoo

cover charge カバーチャージ kabaa chaaji

crash v (car) ぶつかります butsukarimasu

cream (ointment) 軟膏 nankoo

credit card クレジットカード kurejitto kaado

crew neck クルーネック kuruu nekku

crib ベビーベッド bebii beddo

crystal 水晶 suishoo

cup カップ kappu

currency 通貨 tsuuka

currency exchange 両替 ryoogae; **~ office** 両替所 ryoogaejo

current account [BE] 当座預金 tooza yokin

customs 税関 zeekan

cut v (hair) カットします katto shimasu

cut n (injury) 傷 kizu

cute 可愛い kawaii

cycling サイクリング saikuringu

D

damage v 壊れます kowaremasu

damaged 壊れた kowareta

dance v 踊ります odorimasu

dance club ダンスクラブ dansu kurabu

dangerous 危ない abunai

dark 暗い kurai

date (calendar) 日付け hizuke

day 日 hi

deaf 耳が聞こえない mimi ga

kikoenai

debit card デビットカード debitto kaado

deck chair デッキチェア dekki chea

declare v 申告します shisnkoku shimasu

decline v (credit card) 拒否します kyohi shimasu

deeply 深く fukaku

degrees (temperature) 度 do

delay v 遅れます okuremasu

delete v 削除します sakujo shimasu

delicatessen デリカテッセン derikatessen

delicious おいしい oishii

denim デニム denimu

dentist 歯医者 haisha

denture 入れ歯 ireba

deodorant デオドラント deodoranto

department store デパート depaato

departure 出発 shuppatsu

deposit v 預けます azukemasu; ~ n (security) 前金 maekin

desert 砂漠 sabaku

detergent 洗剤 senzai

diabetic 糖尿病 toonyoobyoo

dial v 電話をかけます denwa o kakemasu

diamond ダイアモンド daiamondo

diaper おむつ omutsu

diarrhea 下痢 geri

diesel ディーゼル diizeru

difficult 難しい muzukashii

digital デジタル dejitaru; ~ camera デジタルカメラ dejitaru kamera; ~ **photo** デジタル写真 dejitaru shashin ~ **print** デジタルカメラプリント dejitaru kamera purinto

dining room 食堂 shokudoo

dinner 食事 shokuji

direction 方向 hookoo

dirty 汚い kitanai

disabled 身体障害者 shintai shoogaisha; ~ **accessible** [BE] バリアフリー設備 baria furii setsubi

disconnect (computer) 接続を切ります setsuzoku o kirimasu

discount 割引 waribiki

dish (kitchen) 食器 shokki

dishwasher 食洗器 shokusen ki

dishwashing liquid 中性洗剤 chuusee senzai

display 表示 hyooji

display case ショーケース shookeesu

disposable 使い捨て tsukaisute

disposable razor 使い捨てカミソリ tsukaisute kamisori

dive v 飛び込みます tobikomimasu

diving equipment 潜水用具 sensui

yoogu

divorce v 離婚します rikon shimasu

dizzy めまいがします memai ga shimasu

doctor 医者 isha

doll 人形 ningyoo

dollar (U.S.) ドル doru

domestic 国内の kokunai no

domestic flight 国内線 kokunaisen

dormitory 寮 ryoo

double bed ダブルベッド daburu beddo

downtown 繁華街 hankagai

dozen ダース daasu

drag lift 抗力浮揚 kooryoku fuyoo

dress (piece of clothing) ワンピース wanpiisu

dress code 服装規定 fukusoo kitee

drink v 飲みます nomimasu; ~ n 飲み物 nomimono

drink menu ドリンクメニュー dorinku menyuu

drinking water 飲料水 inryoosui

drive v 運転します unten shimasu

driver's license 運転免許証 unten menkyoshoo; ~ **number** 運転免許証番号 unten menkyoshoo bangoo

drop (medicine) 一滴 itteki

drowsiness 眠気 nemuke

dry cleaner ドライクリーニング店

dorai kuriiningu ten

during …の間 …no aida

duty (tax) 関税 kanzee

duty-free 免税 menzee

DVD DVD dii bui dii

E

ear 耳 mimi

earache 耳の痛み mimi no itami

early 早い hayai

earrings イヤリング iyaringu

east 東 higashi

easy やさしい yasashii

eat v 食べます tabemasu

economy class エコノミークラス ekonomii kurasu

elbow 肘 hiji

electric outlet コンセント konsento

elevator エレベーター erebeetaa

e-mail v メールします meeru shimasu; ~ n 電子メール denshi meeru

e-mail address 電子メールアドレス denshi meeru adoresu

emergency 緊急 kinkyuu

emergency exit 非常口 hijoo guchi

empty v 空にします kara ni shimasu

end v 終わります owarimasu

English (language) 英語 eego

English (people) イギリス人 igirisujin

engrave v 彫り込みます horikomimasu

enjoy v 楽しみます tanoshimimasu

enter v 入ります hairimasu; **(computer)** 入力します nyuuryoku shimasu

entertainment エンターテインメント entaateenmento

entrance 入口 iriguchi

envelope 封筒 fuutoo

equipment 道具 doogu

escalator エスカレーター esuka-reetaa

e-ticket Eチケット i chiketto

evening 夕方 yuugata

excess 超過 chooka

exchange v **(money)** 両替します ryoogae shimasu; ~ v **(goods)** 取り替えます torikaemasu; ~ n **(place)** 交換所 kookanjo

exchange rate (為替)レート (kawase) reeto

excursion エクスカーション ekusu-kaashon

excuse v 許します yurushimasu

exhausted 疲れている tsukareteiru

exit v 出ます demasu; ~ n 出口 deguchi

expensive 高い takai

expert (skill level) 専門家 senmonka

exposure (film) …枚撮り… maitori

express (mail) 速達 sokutatsu; **(train)** 急行 kyuukoo

extension (phone) 内線 naisen

extra 特別な tokubetsuna

extra large 特大 tokudai

extract v **(tooth)** 抜きます nukimasu

eye 目 me

F

face 顔 kao

facial フェーシャル feesharu

family 家族 kazoku

fan (appliance) 扇風機 senpuuki

far 遠い tooi

far-sighted 遠視の enshi no

farm 農家 nooka

fast 速い hayai

fast food ファーストフード faasuto fuudo

fat free 無脂肪 mushiboo

father (one's own) 父 chichi; **(someone else's)** お父さん otoosan

fax v ファックスします fakkusu shimasu; ~ n ファックス fakkusu

fax number ファックス番号 fakkusu bangoo

fee 費用 hiyoo

feed v 授乳します junyuu shimasu

ferry フェリー ferii

fever 熱 netsu

field (sports) フィールド fiirudo

fill up v (food) 満タンにします mantan ni shimasu

fill out v (form) 記入します kinyuu shimasu

filling (tooth) 詰物 tsumemono

film (camera) フイルム fuirumu

fine (fee) 罰金 bakkin

finger 指 yubi

fingernail 爪 tsume

fire 火 hi

fire department 消防署 shooboosho

fire door 耐火扉 taika tobira

first 最初の saisho no

first class ファーストクラス faasuto kurasu

fish 魚 sakana

fit (clothing) 合います aimasu

fitting room 試着室 shichakushitsu

fix v (repair) 直します naoshi masu

flashlight 懐中電灯 kaichuu dentoo

flight 便 bin

floor 階 kai

flower 花 hana

folk music フォークミュージック fooku myuujikku

food 食物 tabemono

foot 足 ashi

football game [BE] サッカーゲーム sakkaa geemu

for (a day) 一日間 ichiinichiikan

forecast 予報 yohoo

foreigner 外国人 gaikokujin

forest 森 mori

fork フォーク fooku

form (fill-in) 用紙 yooshi

formula (baby) フォーミュラ foomyura

fountain 噴水 funsui

free (not busy) 暇 hima; ~ (available) 空いています aitei-masu;

free (no charge) 無料 muryoo

freezer 冷凍庫 reetooko

fresh 新しい atarashii

friend 友人 yuujin

frying pan フライパン furaipan

full-service 完全サービス kanzen saabisu

G

game ゲーム geemu

garage 修理工場 shuurikoojoo

garbage bag ごみ袋 gomibukuro

gas ガソリン gasorin

gas station ガソリンスタンド gasorin sutando

gate (airport) ゲート geeto

gay bar ゲイバー gei baa
gay club ゲイクラブ gei kurabu
gel (hair) ジェル jeru
get to 着きます tsukimasu
get off (a train/bus/subway) 下ります orimasu
gift 贈り物 okurimono
gift shop 売店 baiten
girl 女の子 onna no ko
girlfriend ガールフレンド gaaru furendo
give v あげます agemasu
glass (drinking) コップ koppu; ~ **(material)** ガラス garasu
glasses 眼鏡 megane
go v **(somewhere)** 行きます ikimasu
gold 金 kin
golf course ゴルフ場 gorufujoo
golf tournament ゴルフトーナメント gorufu toonamento
good 良い ii; **(food)** おいしい oishii
good afternoon こんにちは konnichiwa
good evening 今晩は konbanwa
good morning お早うございます ohayoo gozaimasu
goodbye さようなら sayoonara
gram グラム guramu
grandchild 孫 mago
grandparent (one's own) 祖父/祖母 sofu/sobo; **(someone else's)** おじいさん／おばあさん ojiisan/obaasan
gray グレー guree
green 緑／グリーン midori/guriin
grocery store 食料品店 shokuryoohinten
ground floor 一階 ikkai
group グループ guruupu
guide n ガイド gaido
guide book ガイドブック gaido bukku
guide dog 盲導犬 moodoo ken
gym トレーニングジム toreeningu jimu
gynecologist 婦人科医 fujinkai

H

hair 髪 kami
hair dryer ヘアドライヤー hea doraiyaa
hair salon 美容院 biyooin
hairbrush ヘアブラシ hea burashi
haircut ヘアカット hea katto
hairspray ヘアスプレー hea supuree
hairstyle ヘアスタイル hea sutairu
hairstylist ヘアスタイリスト hea sutairisuto
half 半分 hanbun
half hour 半時間 han jikan

half-kilo 半キロ han kiro

hammer ハンマー hanmaa

hand 手 te

hand luggage [BE] 手荷物 tenimotsu

handbag [BE] ハンドバッグ hando baggu

handicapped 身体障害者 shintai shoogaisha

handicapped-accessible ハンディキャップ用 handikyappuyoo

hangover 二日酔い futsuka yoi

happy 楽しい tanoshii

hat 帽子 booshi

have v あります arimasu

head (body part) 頭 atama

headache 頭痛 zutsuu

headphones ヘッドフォン heddofon

health 健康 kenkoo

health food store 健康食品店 kenkoo shokuhinten

heart 心臓 shinzoo

heart condition 心臓病 shinzoobyoo

heat 熱 netsu

heater 暖房 danboo

heating [BE] ヒーター／暖房 hiitaa/danboo

hello こんにちは konnichiwa; **(on the phone)** もしもし moshi moshi

helme ヘルメット herumetto

help 助け tasuke

here ここ koko

hi どうも doomo

high 高い takai

highchair ハイチェアー haicheaa

highway ハイウェー haiuee

hill 丘 oka

hire v **[BE]** 借ります karimasu

hire car **[BE]** レンタカー rentakaa

hitchhike v ヒッチハイクします hitchi haiku shimasu

hockey ホッケー hokkee

holiday [BE] 休日 kyuujitsu

horse track 競馬場 keebajoo

hospital 病院 byooin

hostel ホステル hosuteru

hot (temperature) 暑い atsui; ~ **(spicy)** 辛い karai

hot spring 温泉 onsen

hot water お湯 oyu

hotel ホテル hoteru

hour 時間 jikan

house 家 ie

household good 家庭用品 katee yoohin

housekeeping services 客室清掃サービス kyakushitsu seesoo saabisu

how どうやって dooyatte

how much (money) いくら ikura; **(quantity)** どのくらい dono kurai

hungry お腹がすいた

onaka ga suita

hurt 痛い itai

husband (one's own) 主人 shujin; **(some one else's)** ご主人 goshujin

I

ibuprofen イブプロフェン ibupurofen

ice 氷 koori

ice hockey アイスホッケー aisu hokkee

icy 氷の koori no

identification 身分証明 mibun shoomee

ill 病気 byooki

include v 含みます fukumimasu

indoor pool 室内プール shitsunai puuru

inexpensive 安い yasui

infected 感染した kansen shita

information (phone) 案内 annai

information desk 受付 uketsuke

inn 旅館 ryokan

insect bite 虫さされ mushi sasare

insect repellent 虫除け mushi yoke

insert v **(on an ATM)** 挿入します／入れます soonyuu shimasu/iremasu

insomnia 不眠症 fuminshoo

instant message インスタント・メッセージ insutanto messeeji

insulin インスリン insurin

insurance 保険 hoken; v 保険を掛けます hoken o kakemasu

insurance card 保険証 hokenshoo

insurance company 保険会社 hoken gaisha

interesting 面白い omoshiroi

international (airport area) 国際 kokusai

international flight 国際線 kokusaisen

international student card 国際学生証 kokusai gakuseishoo

internet インターネット intaanetto

internet cafe インターネットカフェ intaanetto kafe

internet service インターネットサービス intaanetto saabisu

interpreter 通訳者 tsuuyakusha

intersection 交差点 koosaten

intestine 腸 choo

introduce v 紹介します shookai shimasu

invoice 請求書 seekyuusho

Ireland アイルランド airurando

Irish アイルランド人 airurando jin

iron v アイロンをかけます airon o kakemasu; ~ n アイロン airon

J

jacket ジャケット jaketto

Japanese (people) 日本人 nihonjin

Japanese (language) 日本語
nihongo

jar 瓶 bin

jaw 顎 ago

jazz ジャズ jazu

jazz club ジャズクラブ jazu kurabu

jeans ジーパン／ジーンズ jiipan/
jiinzu

jeweler 宝石店 hoosekiten

jewelry 宝石 hooseki

join v 加入します kanyuu shimasu

joint (body part) 関節 kansetsu

K

key 鍵 kagi

key card キーカード kii kaado

key ring キーホルダー kii horudaa

kiddie pool 子供用プール
kodomoyoo puuru

kidney (body part) 腎臓 jinzoo

kilogram キロ(グラム) kiro
(guramu)

kilometer キロ(メートル) kiro
(meetoru)

kiss v キスします kisu shimasu

kitchen 台所 daidokoro; ~ foil
[BE] アルミフォイル arumifoiru

knee 膝 hiza

knife ナイフ naifu

L

lace レース reesu

lacquerware 漆器 shikki

lactose intolerant 乳糖不耐症
nyuutoo futaishoo

lake 湖 mizuumi

large 大きい ookii

last 最後 saigo

late (time) 遅い osoi

later あとで atode

launderette [BE] コインランドリ
ー koin randorii

laundromat コインランドリー koin
randorii

laundry 洗濯 sentaku

laundry facility 洗濯施設 sentaku
shisetsu

laundry service ランドリーサービ
ス randorii saabisu

lawyer 弁護士 bengoshi

leather 皮 kawa

leave v 出ます demasu

left (direction) 左 hidari

leg 脚 ashi

lens レンズ renzu

less もっと少ない motto sukunai

lesson レッスン ressun

letter 手紙 tegami

library 図書館 toshokan

life boat 救命ボート kyuumee
booto

life jacket 救命胴衣 kyuumee dooi

lifeguard ライフガード raifu gaado

lift リフト rifuto; ~ **[BE]** エレベーター erebeetaa

lift pass リフト券 rifuto ken

light (overhead) 電灯 dentoo; ~ v **(cigarette)** 火をつけます hi o tsukemasu

lightbulb 電球 denkyuu

lighter ライター raitaa

like v 好きです sukidesu

line (train) 線 sen

linen 麻 asa

lip 唇 kuchibiru

liquor store 酒屋 sakaya

liter リットル rittoru

little 少し／ちょっと sukoshi/chotto

live v 住みます sumimasu

liver (body part) 肝臓 kanzoo

loafers ローファー roofaa

local 地方 chihoo

lock v 鍵をかけます kagi o kakemasu; ~ n 鍵 kagi

locker ロッカー rokkaa

log on ログオンします roggu on shimasu

log off ログオフします roggu ofu shimasu

long 長い nagai

long sleeves 長袖 nagasode

long-sighted [BE] 遠視 enshi

look v 見ます mimasu

lose v **(something)** なくします nakushimasu

lost 道に迷いました michi ni mayoi mashita

lost and found お忘れ物承り所 owasure mono uketamawari jo

lotion ローション rooshon

louder もっと大きい声で motto ookii koe de

love 愛 ai

low 低い hikui

luggage 荷物 nimotsu

luggage cart カート kaato

luggage locker コインロッカー koin rokkaa

luggage ticket 荷物引換券 nimotsu hikikae ken

lunch 昼食 chuushoku

lung 肺 hai

M

magazine 雑誌 zasshi

magnificent 立派 rippa

mail v 郵送します yuusoo shimasu; ~ n 手紙 tegami

mailbox 郵便ポスト yuubin posuto

main attraction メインイベント mein ibento

main course メインコース mein koosu

make up a prescription [BE] 調合します choogoo shimasu

mall ショッピングモール shoppingu mooru

man 男の人 otoko no hito

manager (restaurant, hotel) 支配人 shihainin; (shop) 店長 tenchoo

manicure マニキュア manikyua

manual car マニュアル manyuaru

map n 地図 chizu

market マーケット maaketto

married 結婚している kekkon shiteiru

marry v 結婚します kekkon shimasu

mass (church service) ミサ misa

massage マッサージ massaaji

match n 試合 shiai

meal 食事 shokuji

measure v (someone) 測ります hakarimasu

measuring cup 計量カップ keeryoo kappu

measuring spoon 計量スプーン keeryoo supuun

mechanic 修理工 shuurikoo

medicine 薬 kusuri

medium (size) 中ぐらい chuugurai

meet v (someone) 待ち合わせます machiawasemasu

meeting 会議 kaigi

meeting room 会議室 kaigishitsu

membership card 会員証 kaiin shoo

memorial (place) 記念館 kinenkan

memory card メモリーカード memorii kaado

mend v 直します naoshimasu

menstrual cramp 生理痛 seiritsuu

menu メニュー menyuu

message メッセージ, ご伝言 messeeji, godengon

meter (parking) 料金メーター ryookin meetaa

microwave 電子レンジ denshi renji

midday [BE] 昼間 hiruma

midnight 真夜中 mayonaka

mileage 距離 kyori

mini-bar ミニバー mini baa

minute 分 fun/pun

missing いなくなる inakunaru

mistake 間違い machigai

mobile phone [BE] 携帯電話 keetai denwa

mobility 移動性 idoosee

money お金 okane

month 月 tsuki

mop モップ moppu

moped モペット mopetto

more もっと motto

morning 朝 asa

mosque 回教寺院 kaikyoo jiin

mother (one's own) 母 haha;

(some one else's) お母さん okaasan

motion sickness 乗物酔い norimono yoi

motor boat モーターボート mootaa booto

motorcycle オートバイ ootobai

motorway [BE] 高速道路 koosoku dooro

mountain 山 yama

mountain bike マウンテンバイク maunten baiku

mousse (hair) ムース muusu

mouth 口 kuchi

movie 映画 eega

movie theater 映画館 eegakan

mug v 襲います osoimasu

muscle 筋肉 kinniku

museum 博物館 hakubutsukan

music 音楽 ongaku

music store 楽器屋 gakkiya

N

nail file ネイルファイル neeru fairu

nail salon ネイルサロン neeru saron

name 名前 namae

napkin ナプキン napukin

nappy [BE] おむつ omutsu

nationality 国籍 kokuseki

nature preserve 自然保護区 shizen hogoku

nauseous 吐き〔

near 近く chika〔

near-sighted

nearby 近く〔

neck 首 kub〔

necklace ネックレ〔

need v 要ります irimasu

newspaper 新聞 shinbun

newsstand キオスク kiosuku

next 次 tsugi

nice すてき suteki

night 夜 yoru

nightclub ナイトクラブ naito kurabu

no いいえ iie

non-alcoholic ノンアルコール non arukooru

non-smoking 禁煙 kin-en

noon 正午 shoogo

north 北 kita

nose 鼻 hana

note [BE] お札 osatsu

notify v 知らせます shirasemasu

novice (skill level) 初心者 shoshin-sha

now 今 ima

number 数字 suuji

nurse 看護士 kangoshi

O

office オフィス ofisu

urs オフィスアワー ofisu

cence [BE] 酒屋 sakaya

l オイル oiru

OK オーケー ookee

old (person) 年寄り toshiyori;
(thing) 古い furui

on the corner 角の kadono

once 一度 ichido

one 一つ hitotsu

one-way (ticket) 片道 katamichi

one-way street 一方通行 ippoo
tsuukoo

only ただ tada

open v 開けます akemasu; ~ adj 開
いている aiteiru

opera オペラ opera

opera house オペラハウス opera
hausu

opposite 向かい mukai

optician 眼鏡店 meganeten

orange (color) オレンジ色 orenji iro

orchestra オーケストラ ookesutora

order v 注文します chuumon
shimasu

outdoor pool 屋外プール okugai
puuru

outside 外 soto

over the counter (medication)
処方箋無し shohoosen nashi

overdone 焼き過ぎ yakisugi

overlook (scenic place)
見晴し台 miharashidai

overnight 夜通し yodooshi

oxygen treatment 酸素治療 sanso
chiryoo

P

p.m. n 午後 gogo (1 p.m.; gogo
ichiji)

pacifier おしゃぶり oshaburi

pack v 詰めます tsumemasu

package 小包 kozutsumi

paddling pool [BE] 子供用プール
kodomoyoo puuru

pad [BE] 生理用ナプキン seeriyoo
napukin

pain 痛み itami

pajamas パジャマ pajama

palace 宮殿 kyuuden

pants ズボン zubon

pantyhose パンスト pansuto

paper 紙 kami

paper towel ペーパータオル
peepaa taoru

paracetamol [BE] アセタミノーフ
エン asetaminoofen

park v 駐車します chuusha shimasu;
~ n 公園 kooen

parking garage 駐車場 chuushajoo

parking lot 駐車場 chuushajoo

parking meter 料金メーター

ryookin meetaa

part (for car) 部品 buhin

part-time パートタイム paato taimu

passenger 乗客 jookyaku

passport パスポート pasupooto

passport control 入国手続き nyuukoku tetsuzuki

password パスワード pasu waado

pastry shop ケーキ屋 keekiya

path 道路 dooro

pay v 払います haraimasu

pay phone 公衆電話 kooshuu denwa

peak (of a mountain) 山頂 sanchoo

pearl 真珠 shinju

pedestrian 歩行者 hokoosha

pediatrician 小児科医 shoonikai

pedicure ペディキュア pedikyua

pen ペン pen

penicillin ペニシリン penishirin

penis ペニス penisu

per につき nitsuki

per day 一日につき ichinichi ni tsuki

per hour 一時間につき ichijikan ni tsuki

per night 一晩につき hitoban ni tsuki

per week 一週間につき isshuukan ni tsuki

perfume 香水 koosui

period (menstrual) 生理 seeri; **~(of time)** 期間 kikan

permit v 許可します kyoka shimasu

petite ペティート petiito

petrol [BE] ガソリン gasorin

petrol station [BE] ガソリンスタンド gasorin sutando

pharmacy 薬局 yakkyoku

phone v 電話します denwa shimasu; ~ n 電話 denwa

phone call 電話 denwa

phone card テレホンカード terehon kaado

phone number 電話番号 denwa bangoo

photo 写真 shashin

photocopy コピー kopii

photography 写真撮影 shashin satsuee

pick up (something) 受け取ります uketorimasu

picnic area ピクニック場 pikunik-kujoo

pill (birth control) ピル piru

pillow 枕 makura

personal identification number (PIN) 暗証番号 anshoo bangoo

pink ピンク pinku

piste [BE] ゲレンデ gerende

piste map [BE] ゲレンデ地図 gerende chizu

pizzeria ピザ・レストラン piza resutoran

place v (a bet) 掛け金を払います kakekin o haraimasu; n 場所 basho

plane 飛行機 hikooki

plastic wrap ラップ rappu

plate 皿 sara

platform ホーム hoomu

platinum プラチナ purachina

play v します shimasu; ~ n (theatre) 芝居 shibai

playground 公園 kooen

playpen ベビーサークル bebii saakuru

please (asking for a favor) お願いします onegai shimasu; (offering a favor) どうぞ doozo

pleasure 楽しみ tanoshimi

plunger トイレの吸引具 toire no kyuuingu

plus size プラスサイズ purasu saizu

pocket ポケット poketto

poison 毒 doku

poles (skiing) ストック sutokku

police 警察 keesatsu

police report 警察の証明書 keesatsu no shoomeesho

police station 交番 kooban

pond 池 ike

pool プール puuru

pop music ポピュラー音楽 popyuraa ongaku

portion 部分 bubun

post [BE] 手紙 tegami

post office 郵便局 yuubinkyoku

postbox [BE] 郵便ポスト yuubin posuto

postcard 葉書 hagaki

pot 深鍋 fukanabe

pottery 陶器 tooki

pound (weight) ポンド pondo; ~ (British sterling) ポンド pondo

pregnant 妊娠 ninshin

prepaid phone プリペイド携帯 puripeedo keetai

prescribe v 処方します shohoo shimasu

prescription 処方箋 shohoosen

press v (clothing) アイロンをかけます airon o kakemasu

price 値段 nedan

print v 印刷します insatsu shimasu

problem 問題 mondai

produce 食料品 shokuryoohin

produce store 食料品店 shokuryoohinten

prohibit v 禁止します kinshi shimasu

pronounce v 発音します hatsuon shimasu

public 公共 kookyoo

pull v 引きます hikimasu

purple 紫 murasaki

purse 財布 saifu

push v押します oshimasu

pushchair [BE] ベビーカー bebii kaa

Q

quality 質 shitsu

question 質問 shitsumon

quiet 静か shizuka

R

racetrack 競馬場 keebajoo

racket (sports) ラケット raketto

railway station [BE] 駅 eki

rain n 雨 ame

raincoat レインコート reinkooto

rainforest 雨林 urin

rainy 雨の ameno

rap (music) ラップ rappu

rape 強姦 gookan

rash 発疹 hasshin

razor blade カミソリの刃 kamisori no ha

reach v届きます todokimasu

ready 用意ができている yooi ga dekite iru

real 本物 honmono

receipt レシート／領収書 reshiito/ ryooshuusho

receive v受け取ります uketorimasu

reception 受付 uketsuke

recharge v充電します juuden shimasu

recommend v推薦します suisen shimasu

recommendation 推薦 suisen

recycling リサイクリング risaikuringu

red 赤い akai

refrigerator 冷蔵庫 reezooko

region 地域 chiiki

registered mail 書留 kakitome

regular レギュラー regyuraa

relationship 関係 kankee

rent v借ります karimasu

rental car レンタカー rentakaa

repair v修理します shuuri shimasu

repeat vもう一度言います moo ichido iimasu

reservation 予約 yoyaku

reservation desk 予約窓口 yoyaku madoguchi

reserve v予約します yoyaku shimasu

restaurant レストラン resutoran

restroom 化粧室 keshooshitsu

retired 退職した taishoku shita

return v返します kaeshimasu; ~ n [BE] 往復 oofuku

rib (body part) 肋骨 rokkotsu

rice cooker 炊飯器 suihanki

right (direction) 右 migi
right of way 優先権 yuusenken
ring 指輪／リング yubiwa/ringu
river 川 kawa
road map 道路地図 dooro chizu
rob v盗みます nusumimasu
robbed 盗まれました nusumare mashita
romantic ロマンチック romanchikku
room 部屋 heya
room key 部屋の鍵 heya no kagi
room service ルームサービス ruumu saabisu
round-trip 往復 oofuku
route コース koosu
rowboat ボート booto
rubbish [BE] ゴミ gomi
rubbish bag [BE] ゴミ袋 gomi bukuro
ruins 遺跡 iseki
rush ラッシュ rasshu

S

sad 悲しい kanashii
safe (thing) 金庫 kinko; ~ **(protected)** 安全 anzen
sales tax 消費税 shoohizee
sandals サンダル sandaru
sanitary napkin 生理用ナプキン seeriyoo napukin

saucepan 鍋 nabe
sauna サウナ sauna
save v(on a computer) 保存します hozon shimasu
savings (account) 普通預金 futsuu yokin
scanner スキャナー sukyanaa
scarf スカーフ sukaafu
schedule v予定に入れます yotee ni iremasu; ~ n 予定 yotee
school 学校 gakkoo
science 科学 kagaku
scissors はさみ hasami
sea 海 umi
seat 席 seki
security 警備 keebi
see v見ます mimasu
self-service セルフサービス serufu saabisu
sell v売ります urimasu
seminar セミナー seminaa
send v送ります okurimasu
senior citizen 高齢者 kooreesha
separated (marriage) 別居 bekkyo
serious 真面目な majimena
service (in a restaurant) サービス saabisu
sexually transmitted disease (STD) 性病 seebyoo
shampoo シャンプー shanpuu
sharp 鋭い surudoi

shaving cream シェービングクリーム sheebingu kuriimu

sheet シーツ shiitsu

ship v (mail) 送ります okurimasu

shirt シャツ shatsu

shoe store 靴屋 kutsuya

shoes 靴 kutsu

shop v 買い物をします kaimono o shimasu

shopping 買い物 kaimono

shopping area 商店街 shooten gai

shopping centre [BE] ショッピングセンター shoppingu sentaa

shopping mall ショッピングモール shoppingu mooru

short 短い mijikai

short sleeves 半袖 hansode

shorts 半ズボン hanzubon

short-sighted [BE] 近視 kinshi

shoulder 肩 kata

show v 見せます misemasu

shower シャワー shawaa

shrine 神社 jinja

sick 病気 byooki

side dish 付け合わせ tsukeawase

side effect 副作用 fukusayoo

sightseeing 観光 kankoo

sightseeing tour 観光ツアー kankoo tsuaa

sign v 署名します／サインします shomeeshimasu/sainshimasu

silk 絹 kinu

silver 銀 gin

single (unmarried) 独身 dokushin

single bed シングルベッド shinguru beddo

single room シングルルーム shinguru ruumu

sink 流し nagashi

sister (my older) 姉 ane

sister (my younger) 妹 imooto

sister (someone else's older) お姉さん oneesan

sister (someone else's younger) 妹さん imootosan

sit v 座ります suwarimasu

size サイズ saizu

skin 皮膚 hifu

skirt スカート sukaato

ski スキー sukii

ski lift スキーリフト sukii rifuto

sleep v 眠ります nemurimasu

sleeper car 寝台車 shindaisha

sleeping bag 寝袋／スリーピングバッグ nebukuro/suriipingu baggu

slice (of something) 一切れ hitokire

slippers スリッパ surippa

slower もっとゆっくり motto yukkuri

slowly ゆっくり yukkuri

small 小さい chiisai

smaller もっと小さい motto chiisai

smoke v 煙草を吸います tabako o suimasu

smoking (area) 喫煙席 kitsuenseki

snack bar スナックバー sunakku baa

sneaker スニーカー suniikaa

snorkeling equipment スノーケル 用具 sunookeru yoogu

snowboard スノーボード sunoo boodo

snowshoe 雪靴 yukigutsu

snowy 雪の多い yuki no ooi

soap 石鹸 sekken

soccer サッカー sakkaa

sock 靴下 kutsushita

soother [BE] おしゃぶり oshaburi

sore throat 喉の痛み nodo no itami

sorry ごめんなさい gomennasai

south 南 minami

souvenir お土産 omiyage

souvenir store お土産屋 omiyageya

spa 温泉 onsen

spatula へら hera

speak v 話します hanashimasu

specialist (doctor) 専門医 senmon-i

specimen 見本 mihon

speeding スピード違反 supiido ihan

spell v つづりを言います tsuzuri o iimasu

spicy 辛い karai

spine (body part) 脊椎 sekitsui

spoon スプーン supuun

sports スポーツ supootsu

sporting goods store スポーツ用 品店 supootsu yoohinten

sprain 捻挫 nenza

stadium スタジアム sutajiamu

stairs 階段 kaidan

stamp n (postage) 切手 kitte

start v (a car) スタートします sutaato shimasu

starter [BE] 前菜 zensai

station 駅 eki

statue 銅像 doozoo

stay v 泊まります tomarimasu

steal v 盗みます nusumimasu

steep 急斜面 kyuushamen

sterling silver 純銀 jungin

sting n 虫さされ mushi sasare

stolen 盗まれた nusumareta

stomach 胃 i

stomachache 腹痛 fukutsuu

stop v 止まります tomarimasu; ~ (bus) n バス停 basu tee

store directory 店内の案内 tennai no annai

storey [BE] 階 kai

stove コンロ konro

straight 真っ直ぐ massugu

strange 変 hen

stream 小川 ogawa

...Street ...通り ...doori

stroller ベビーカー bebiikaa

student 学生 gakusee

study v 勉強します benkyoo shimasu

stunning 驚くほどの odoroku hodono

subtitle (movie) 字幕 jimaku

subway 地下鉄 chikatetsu

subway station 地下鉄の駅 chika-tetsu no eki

suit スーツ suutsu

suitcase スーツケース suutsu keesu

sun 太陽 taiyoo

sunblock 日焼け止めクリーム hiyakedome kuriimu

sunburn 日焼け hiyake

sunglasses サングラス sangurasu

sunny 晴れの hareno

sunscreen 日除け hiyoke

sunstroke 日射病 nisshabyoo

super (fuel) スーパー suupaa

supermarket スーパー suupaa

surfboard サーフボード saafu boodo

sushi restaurant 寿司屋 sushi ya

swallow v 呑み込みます nomikomimasu

sweater セーター seetaa

sweatshirt トレーナー toreenaa

sweet (taste) 甘い amai

sweets [BE] キャンデー kyandee

swelling 腫れ hare

swim v 泳ぎます oyogimasu

swimsuit 水着 mizugi

symbol (keyboard) 記号 kigoo

synagogue ユダヤ教会 yudaya kyookai

T

table テーブル teeburu

tablet (medicine) 錠 joo

take v (medicine) 飲みます nomimasu

take away [BE] テークアウト teeku auto

tampon タンポン tanpon

taste v 味がします aji ga shimasu

taxi タクシー takushii

tea お茶 ocha

team チーム chiimu

teahouse 喫茶店 kissaten

teaspoon 茶匙 chasaji

telephone 電話 denwa

temple (religious) お寺 otera; ~ accommodation 宿坊 shukuboo

temporary 一時的 ichijiteki

tennis テニス tenisu

tent テント tento

tent peg テント用ペグ tento yoo

pegu

tent pole テントの支柱 tento no shichuu

terminal (airport) ターミナル taaminaru

terracotta テラコッタ terakotta

terrible ひどい hidoi

text v **(send a message)** メールを送ります meeru o okurimasu; ~ n **(message)** メール meeru

thank v 感謝します kansha shimasu

thank you ありがとう arigatoo

thank you (for food) ごちそうさまでした gochisoo sama deshita

that あれ are

theater 劇場 gekijoo

theft 盗難 toonan

there そこ soko

thief 泥棒 doroboo

thigh 腿 momo

thirsty 喉が渇きました nodo ga kawaki mashita

this これ kore

throat 喉 nodo

ticket 切符 kippu

ticket office 切符売り場 kippu uriba

tie (clothing) ネクタイ nekutai

time 時間 jikan

timetable [BE] 時刻表 jikokuhyoo

tire タイヤ taiya

tired 疲れました tsukare mashita

tissue ティッシュペーパー tisshu peepaa

tobacconist 煙草屋 tabakoya

today 今日 kyoo

toe 足指 ashi yubi

toenail 足の爪 ashi no tsume

toilet [BE] 化粧室 keshooshitsu

toilet paper トイレットペーパー toiretto peepaa

tomorrow あした ashita

tongue 舌 shita

tonight 今晩 konban

too …過ぎます …sugimasu

tooth 歯 ha

toothpaste 歯磨き粉 hamigakiko

total (amount) 合計 gookee

tough (food) 硬い katai

tourist 観光客 kankookyaku

tourist information office 観光案内所 kankoo annaijo

tour ツアー tsuaa

tow truck レッカー車 rekkaasha

towel タオル taoru

tower 塔 too

town 町 machi

town hall 市役所 shiyakusho

town map 市街地図 shigai chizu

town square 町の広場 machi no hiroba

toy 玩具 omocha

toy store 玩具屋 omochaya

track (train) 路線 rosen

traditional 伝統的 dentooteki

traffic light 信号 shingoo

trail 道 michi

trail map ハイキングコース案内 haikingu koosu annai

train 列車 ressha; **(commuter train)** 電車 densha

train station 駅 eki

transfer v **(change trains/ flights)** 乗り換えます norikae masu; ~ v **(money)** 送金します sookin shimasu

translate v翻訳します hon-yaku shimasu

trash ゴミ gomi

travel agency 旅行代理店 ryokoo dairiten

travel sickness 乗物酔い norimono yoi

traveler's check トラベラーズチェック toraberaazu chekku

traveller's cheque [BE] トラベラーズチェック toraberaazu chekku

tree 木 ki

trim v **(hair)** そろえます soroemasu

trip 旅行 ryokoo

trolley [BE] カート kaato

trousers [BE] ズボン zubon

T-shirt Tシャツ tii shatsu

turn off (lights) 消します keshimasu

turn on (lights) つけます tsukemasu

TV テレビ terebi

type vタイプします taipu shimasu

tyre [BE] タイヤ taiya

U

United Kingdom (U.K.) イギリス igirisu

United States (U.S.) アメリカ amerika

ugly みにくい minikui

umbrella 傘 kasa

unattended 無人の mujinno

unconscious 意識不明の ishiki fumeeno

underground [BE] 地下鉄 chikatetsu

underground station [BE] 地下鉄の駅 chikatetsu no eki

underpants [BE] パンツ pantsu

understand v分かります wakari masu

underwear 下着 shitagi

university 大学 daigaku

unleaded (gas) 無鉛 muen

upper 上の ueno

urgent 緊急 kinkyuu

use v使います / 利用します tsukai masu/riyoo shimasu

username ユーザー名 yuuzaa mee

utensil 器具 kigu

V

vacancy 空き室 akishitsu

vacation 休暇 kyuuka

vaccination 予防接種 yoboo sesshu

vacuum cleaner 電気掃除機 denki soojiki

vagina 膣 chitsu

vaginal infection 膣炎 chitsuen

valid 有効 yuukoo

valley 谷間 tanima

valuable 貴重な kichoona

value 値段 nedan

vegetarian ベジタリアン bejitarian

vehicle registration 自動車登録証 jidoosha toorokushoo

viewpoint [BE] 展望台 tenboodai

village 村 mura

vineyard ぶどう園 budooen

visa ビザ biza

visit v 訪れます otozure masu

visiting hours 開館時間 kaikan jikan

visually impaired 視覚障害者 shikaku shoogaisha

vitamin ビタミン bitamin

V-neck ブイネック bui nekku

volleyball game バレーボール試合 bareebooru shiai

vomit v 吐きます hakimasu

W

wait v 待ちます machimasu; ~ n 待ち時間 machi jikan

waiter ウェーター ueetaa

waiting room 待合室 machiaishitsu

waitress ウェートレス ueetoresu

wake v 起こします okoshi masu

wake-up call モーニングコール mooningu kooru

walk v 歩きます aruki masu; ~ n 散歩 sanpo

walking route 散歩道 sanpomichi

wall clock 柱時計 hashira dokee

wallet 財布 saifu

warm v (something) 暖めます atatame masu; ~ adj (temperature) 暖かい atatakai

washing machine 洗濯機 sentakuki

watch 腕時計 ude dokee

water 水 mizu

water skis 水上スキー suijoo sukii

waterfall 滝 taki

weather 天気 tenki

week 週 shuu

weekend 週末 shuumatsu

weekly 毎週 maishuu

welcome v 歓迎します kangee shimasu

well-rested よく休みました yoku yasumi mashita

west 西 nishi

what 何 nani

wheelchair 車椅子 kuruma isu

wheelchair ramp 車椅子用スロープ kuruma isu yoo suroopu

when いつ itsu

where どこ doko

white 白い shiroi

who 誰 dare

widowed 夫と死別した otto to shibetsu shita

wife (one's own) 家内 kanai; **(someone else's)** 奥さん okusan

window 窓 mado; ~ **(on flight)** 窓側 madogawa; **by the ~** 窓際 madogiwa

wine list ワインリスト wain risuto

winter 冬 fuyu

wireless internet ワイアレスインターネット waiaresu intaanetto

wireless internet service ワイアレスインターネット サービス waiaresu intaanetto saabisu

wireless phone 携帯電話 keetai denwa

with (attached) …付き tsuki; **(included)** …込み komi

withdraw v 引き出します hikidashi masu

withdrawal (bank) 引き出し hikidashi

without 無しで nashide

woman 女性 josee

wool ウール uuru

work v 働きます hataraki masu

wrap v **(a package)** 包みます tsutsumi masu

wrist 手首 tekubi

write v 書きます kaki masu

Y

year 年 toshi

yellow 黄色 kiiro

yen 円 en

yes はい hai

yesterday 昨日 kinoo

young 若い wakai

you're welcome どういたしまして doo itashi mashite

youth hostel ユースホステル yuusu hosuteru

Z

zero ゼロ / 零 zero/ree

zoo 動物園 doobutsuen

Japanese–English

194

A

aakeedo アーケード arcade

abunai 危ない dangerous

adaputa アダプタ adapter

afutaa sheebu アフターシェーブ aftershave

agemasu あげます v give

ago 顎 jaw

ai 愛 love

aida 間 during

aimasu 合います fit (clothing)

airon アイロン iron

airon o kakemasu アイロンをかけます v iron (clothing)

airurando アイルランド Ireland

airurando jin アイルランド人 Irish

aisu hokkee アイスホッケー ice hockey

aiteimasu 空いています free (available)

aiteiru 開いている adj open

aji ga shimasu 味がします v taste

aji ga usui 味が薄い bland

ajia no アジアの Asian

akai 赤い red

akachan 赤ちゃん baby

akari 明かり light (overhead)

akemasu 開けます v open

akishitsu 空き室 vacancy

akusesarii アクセサリー accessories

akusesu shimasu アクセスします v access (Internet)

amai 甘い sweet (taste)

ame 雨 rain

ameno 雨の rainy

amerika no アメリカの American

amerika アメリカ United States (U.S.)

ane 姉 sister (my older)

ani 兄 brother (my older)

annai 案内 information (phone)

anshoo bangoo 暗証番号 personal identification number (PIN)

anzen 安全 safe (protected)

are あれ that

arerugii hannoo アレルギー反応 allergic reaction

arerugii アレルギー allergic

arigatoo ありがとう thank you

arimasu あります v have

aroma serapii アロマセラピー aromatherapy

aruki masu 歩きます v walk

arumi hoiru アルミホイル aluminum foil

asa 朝 morning

asa 麻 linen

asetaminoofen アセタミノーフェン

paracetamol [BE]

ashi no tsume 足の爪 toenail

ashi 脚 leg

ashi 足 foot

ashikubi 足首 ankle

ashita あした tomorrow

atama 頭 head (body part)

atarashii 新しい fresh

atatakai 暖かい *adj* warm
(temperature)

atatame masu 暖めます *v* warm
(something)

ato 後 after

atode あとで later

atorakushon アトラクショ
ン attraction (place)

atsui 暑い hot (temperature)

azukemasu 預けます *v* deposit
(money); check (luggage)

B

baa バー bar (place)

baggu バッグ bag

baiten 売店 gift shop

bakkin 罰金 fine (fee)

baree バレエ ballet

bareebooru no shiai バレーボール
の試合 volleyball game

baria furii setsubi バリアフリー設
備 disabled accessible [BE]

basho 場所 *n* place

basu バス bus

basu no kippu バスの切符 bus
ticket

basu ryokoo バス旅行 bus tour

basu taaminaru バスターミナ
ル bus station

basu teeryuujo バス停留所 bus
stop

basuketto booru バスケットボー
ル basketball

basutee バス停 bus stop

bebii beddo ベビーベッド crib

bebii kaa ベビーカー pushchair
[BE]

bebii saakuru ベビーサーク
ル playpen

bebii shittaa ベビーシッタ
ー babysitter

beddo ベッド bed

beeju ベージュ beige

bejitarian ベジタリアン vegetarian

bekkyo 別居 separated (marriage)

bengoshi 弁護士 lawyer

benjo 便所 restroom (informal)/
toilet [BE] (informal)

benkyoo shimasu 勉強します *v*
study

benpi 便秘 constipated

beruto ベルト belt

biichi ビーチ beach

bijinesu kurasu ビジネス・クラ

ス business class
bijinesu sentaa ビジネス・センター business center
bikini ビキニ bikini
bin 便 flight
bin 瓶 jar
biru ビル building
bitamin ビタミン vitamin
biyooin 美容院 hair salon
biza ビザ visa
boku 僕 I (male, informal)
bonyuu o agemasu 母乳をあげます breastfeed
booi furendo ボーイフレンド boyfriend
bookoo 膀胱 bladder
booru ボール bowl
booshi 帽子 hat
booto ボート rowboat
bubun 部分 portion
budooen ぶどう園 vineyard
buhin 部品 part (for car)
bui nekku ブイネック V-neck
burajaa ブラジャー bra
burausu ブラウス blouse
bureeki ブレーキ brakes (car)
buresuretto ブレスレット bracelet
buriifu ブリーフ briefs
buroochi ブローチ brooch
buruu ブルー blue
butsukarimasu ぶつかります v

crash (car)
buutsu ブーツ boots
byooin 病院 hospital
byooki 病気 sick

C

chairo 茶色 brown
chairudo shiito チャイルドシート car seat
chasaji 茶匙 teaspoon
chekku チェック check
chekku auto チェックアウト checkout (hotel)
chekku in チェックイン check-in
chibusa 乳房 breast
chichi 父 father (one's own)
chihoo 地方 local
chiiki 地域 region
chiimu チーム team
chiisai 小さい small
chikai 近い close
chikaku 近く nearby
chikatetsu 地下鉄 subway/underground [BE]
chikatetsu no eki 地下鉄の駅 subway station/underground [BE] station
chitsu 膣 vagina
chitsuen 膣炎 vaginal infection
chizu 地図 n map
choo 腸 intestine

choogoo shimasu 調合します v fill/ make up [BE] (a prescription)

chooka 超過 excess

chooshoku 朝食 breakfast

chotto ちょっと little

chuugurai 中ぐらい medium (size)

chuumon shimasu 注文します v order

chuusee senzai 中性洗剤 dishwashing liquid

chuusha shimasu 駐車します v park

chuushajoo 駐車場 parking garage/ car park [BE]

chuushoku 昼食 lunch

D

daasu ダース dozen

daburu beddo ダブルベッド double bed

daiamondo ダイアモンド diamond

daidokoro 台所 kitchen

daigaku 大学 university

dainingu ruumu ダイニングルーム dining room

dairiten 代理店 agency

daiseedoo 大聖堂 cathedral

danboo 暖房 heater/heating [BE]

dansu kurabu ダンスクラブ dance club

dare 誰 who

debitto kaado デビットカード debit card

deguchi 出口 exit

dejitaru デジタル digital

dejitaru kamera デジタルカメラ digital camera

dejitaru kamera purinto デジタルカメラプリント digital print

dejitaru shashin デジタル写真 digital photo

dekki chea デッキチェア deck chair

demasu 出ます v leave

denchi 電池 battery

denimu デニム denim

denki soojiki 電気掃除機 vacuum cleaner

denkyuu 電球 lightbulb

densensee 伝染性 contagious

densha 電車 train (commuter train)

denshi meeru 電子メール e-mail

denshi meeru adoresu 電子メールアドレス e-mail address

denshi renji 電子レンジ microwave

dentoo 電灯 light (overhead)

dentooteki 伝統的 traditional

denwa 電話 telephone

denwa bangoo 電話番号 phone number

denwa o kakemasu 電話をかけます v dial

denwa shimasu 電話します v

phone

deodoranto デオドラント
deodorant

depaato デパート　department store

derikatessen デリカテッセン
delicatessen

dii bui dii DVD　DVD

diizeru ディーゼル　diesel

do 度　degrees (temperature)

dochira どちら　which (polite)

doki 土器　clay pot

doko どこ　where

doku 毒　poison

dokushin 独身　single (unmarried)

dono kurai どのくらい　how much
(quantity)

doo 銅　copper

doo itashi mashite どういたしまし
て　you're welcome

doobutsu 動物　animal

doobutsuen 動物園　zoo

doogu 道具　equipment

dookutsu 洞窟　cave

doomo どうも　hi

doomyaku 動脈　artery

…doori …通り　…Street

dooro 道路　path

dooro chizu 道路地図　road map

dooryoo 同僚　colleague

dooyatte どうやって　how

doozo どうぞ　please (offering a favor)

doozoo 銅像　statue

dorai kuriiningu ten ドライクリーニ
ング店　dry cleaner

dorinku menyuu ドリンクメニュ
ー　drink menu

doroboo 泥棒　thief

doru ドル　dollar (U.S.)

dotchi どっち　which

E

eakon エアコン　air conditioning

eaponpu エアポンプ　air pump

eega 映画　movie

eegakan 映画館　movie theater

eego 英語　English (language)

eegyoo jikan 営業時間　business
hours

eekokujin 英国人　British

eetiiemu キャッシュコーナー　ATM

eezu エイズ　AIDS

eki 駅　train station/railway station
[BE]

ekonomii kurasu エコノミークラス
economy class

ekusukaashon エクスカーション
excursion

en 円　yen

enshi 遠視　far-sighted/long-sighted
[BE]

erebeetaa エレベーター　elevator/
lift [BE]

esukareetaa エスカレーター escalator

F

faasuto fuudo ファーストフード fast food

faasuto kurasu ファーストクラス first class

fakkusu ファックス fax

fakkusu bangoo ファックス番号 fax number

fakkusu shimasu ファックスします v fax

feesharu フェーシャル facial

ferii フェリー ferry

fiirudo フィールド field (sports)

fooku フォーク fork

fooku myuujikku フォークミュージック folk music

fuirumu フィルム film (camera)

fujinkai 婦人科医 gynecologist

fukaku 深く deeply

fukanabe 深鍋 pot

fukumimasu 含みます v include

fukusayoo 副作用 side effect

fukusoo kitee 服装規定 dress code

fukutsuu 腹痛 stomachache

fuminshoo 不眠症 insomnia

fun 分 minute

funsui 噴水 fountain

furaipan フライパン frying pan

furoba 風呂場 bathroom

furui 古い old (thing)

futsuka yoi 二日酔い hangover

futsuu yokin 普通預金 savings (account)

fuutoo 封筒 envelope

fuyu 冬 winter

G

gaaru furendo ガールフレンド girlfriend

gaido ガイド n guide

gaido bukku ガイドブック guide book

gaikokujin 外国人 foreigner

gake 崖 cliff

gakkiya 楽器屋 music store

gakkoo 学校 school

gakusee 学生 student

gamu ガム chewing gum

garasu ガラス glass (material)

gasorin ガソリン gas/petrol [BE]

gasorin sutando ガソリンスタンド gas station/petrol station [BE]

gasu ガス cooking gas

geemu ゲーム game

geeto ゲート gate (airport)

gei baa ゲイバー gay bar

gei kurabu ゲイクラブ gay club

gekijoo 劇場 theater

genkin 現金 cash

gerende ゲレンデ trail/piste [BE]

gerende chizu ゲレンデ地図 trail/piste [BE] map

geri 下痢 diarrhea

gifuto shoppu ギフトショップ gift shop

gin 銀 silver

ginkoo 銀行 bank

gochisoo sama deshita ごちそうさまでした thank you (for food)

godengon ご伝言 message

gogo 午後 afternoon/p.m.

gomen kudasai ごめんください bye

gomennasai ごめんなさい sorry

gomi ゴミ trash/rubbish [BE]

gomi bukuro ゴミ袋 garbage bag/rubbish bag [BE]

gookan 強姦 rape

gookee 合計 total (amount)

gorufu toonamento ゴルフトーナメント golf tournament

gorufujoo ゴルフ場 golf course

goshujin ご主人 husband (someone else's)

gozen 午前 a.m.

guramu グラム gram

gurasu グラス glass (drinking)

guree グレー gray

guriin グリーン green

guruupu グループ group

H

ha 歯 tooth

hagaki 葉書 postcard

haha 母 mother (one's own)

hai はい yes

hai 肺 lung

haicheaa ハイチェアー highchair

haiiro 灰色 gray

haikingu koosu annai ハイキングコース案内 trail/piste [BE] map

hairimasu 入ります v enter

haisha 歯医者 dentist

haiuee ハイウェー highway

hajime masu 始めます v begin

hakarimasu 測ります v measure (someone)

hakike 吐き気 nauseous

hakimasu 吐きます v vomit

hako 箱 box

hakubutsukan 博物館 museum

hamaki 葉巻 cigar

hamigakiko 歯磨き粉 toothpaste

han jikan 半時間 half hour

han kiro 半キロ half-kilo

hana 花 flower

hana 鼻 nose

hanashimasu 話します v speak

hanbun 半分 half

handi kyappuyoo ハンディキャップ

用 handicapped-accessible

hando baggu ハンドバッグ purse/handbag [BE]

hankagai 繁華街 downtown

hanmaa ハンマー hammer

hansode 半袖 short sleeves

hanzubon 半ズボン shorts

haraimasu 払います v pay

hare 腫れ swelling

hareno 晴れの sunny

hari 鍼 acupuncture

hasami はさみ scissors

hashi 橋 bridge

hashira dokee 柱時計 wall clock

hasshin 発疹 rash

hatarakimasu 働きます v work

hatsuon shimasu 発音します v pronounce

hayai 早い early

hayai 速い fast

hea burashi ヘアブラシ hairbrush

hea doraiyaa ヘアドライヤー hair dryer

hea katto ヘアカット haircut

hea supuree ヘアスプレー hairspray

hea sutairisuto ヘアスタイリスト hairstylist

hea sutairu ヘアスタイル hairstyle

heddofoon ヘッドフォーン headphones

heekan 閉館 closed

heeten 閉店 closed

hen 変 strange

henkoo 変更 change (plan)

hera へら spatula

herumetto ヘルメット helmet

heya 部屋 room

heya no kagi 部屋の鍵 room key

hi o tsukemasu 火をつけます v light (cigarette)

hi 日 day

hi 火 fire

hidari 左 left (direction)

hifu 皮膚 skin

higashi 東 east

hiitaa ヒーター heater/heating [BE]

hiji 肘 elbow

hijoo guchi 非常口 emergency exit

hikidashi 引き出し withdrawal (bank)

hikidashi masu 引き出します v withdraw

hikkimasu 引きます v pull

hikooki 飛行機 airplane

hikui 低い low

hima 暇 free (not busy)

hinketsu no 貧血の anemic

hiruma 昼間 noon/midday [BE]

hitchi haiku shimasu ヒッチハイク します v hitchhike

hitoban ni tsuki 一晩につき per

night

hitokire 一切れ slice (of something)

hitori 一人 alone

hitotsu 一つ one

hiyake 日焼け sunburn

hiyakedome kuriimu 日焼け止めクリーム sunblock

hiyoke 日除け sunscreen

hiyoo 費用 fee

hiza 膝 knee

hizuke 日付け date (calendar)

hoka no michi 他の道 alternate route

hoken 保険 insurance

hoken gaisha 保険会社 insurance company

hoken o kakemasu 保険を掛けます v insure

hokenshoo 保険証 insurance card

hokkee ホッケー hockey

hokoosha 歩行者 pedestrian

hon 本 book

hone 骨 bone

honmono 本物 real

hon-ya 本屋 bookstore

hon-yaku shimasu 翻訳します v translate

honyuubin 哺乳瓶 baby bottle

hooki 箒 broom

hookoo 方向 direction

hoomu ホーム platform

hooseki 宝石 jewelry

hoosekiten 宝石店 jeweler

hootai 包帯 bandage

horikomimasu 彫り込みます v engrave

hoshiin desuga 欲しいんですが I'd like…

hosuteru ホステル hostel

hoteru ホテル hotel

hozon shimasu 保存します v save (on a computer)

hyooji 表示 display

I

i 胃 stomach

ibupurofen イブプロフェン ibuprofen

ichiban ii 一番いい best

ichido 一度 once

ichiinichiikan 一日間 for (a day)

ichijikan ni tsuki 一時間につき per hour

ichijiteki 一時的 temporary

ichinichi ni tsuki 一日につき per day

idoosee 移動性 mobility

ie 家 house

igirisu イギリス United Kingdom (U.K.)

igirisujin イギリス人 English

ii 良い good

iichiketto Eチケット e-ticket

iie いいえ no
ike 池 pond
iki 行き bound
iki masu 行きます v go
ikkai 一階 ground floor
ikura いくら how much (money)
ima 今 now
imooto 妹 sister (my younger)
imootosan 妹さん sister (someone else's younger)
inakunaru いなくなる missing
inryoosui 飲料水 drinking water
insatsu shimasu 印刷します v print
insurin インスリン insulin
insutanto messeeji インスタント・メッセージ instant message
intaanetto インターネット internet
intaanetto kafe インターネットカフェ internet cafe
intaanetto saabisu インターネットサービス internet service
ippoo tsuukoo 一方通行 one-way street
ireba 入れ歯 denture
iremasu 入れます v insert (on an ATM)
iriguchi 入口 entrance
irimasu 要ります v need
iro 色 color
irui 衣類 clothing
iseki 遺跡 ruins

isha 医者 doctor
ishiki fumeino 意識不明の unconscious
ishitsubutu gakari 遺失物係 lost and found
issho 一緒 together
isshuukan ni tsuki 一週間につき per week
isu 椅子 chair
itai 痛い hurt
itami 痛み pain
itsu いつ when
itteki 一滴 drop (medicine)
iyaringu イヤリング earrings

J

jaketto ジャケット jacket
jazu ジャズ jazz
jazu kurabu ジャズクラブ jazz club
jeru ジェル gel (hair)
jidoo 自動 automatic
jidoosha toorokushoo 自動車登録証 vehicle registration
jiinzu ジーンズ jeans
jikan 時間 hour/time
jiko 事故 accident
jikokuhyoo 時刻表 timetable [BE]
jimaku 字幕 subtitle (movie)
jinja 神社 shrine
jinzoo 腎臓 kidney (body part)
jitensha 自転車 bicycle

jitensha ruuto 自転車ルート bike route

joo 錠 tablet (medicine)

jookyaku 乗客 passenger

joosha shimasu 乗車します v board (train)

josee 女性 woman

jungin 純銀 sterling silver

junyuu shimasu 授乳します v feed (baby)

juuden shimasu 充電します v recharge

juusho 住所 address

K

kaado カード card

kaado de haraimasu カードで払います v charge (credit card)

kaato カート cart/trolley [BE]

kaaton カートン carton

kabaa chaaji カバーチャージ cover charge

kado no 角の on the corner

kado o magatta tokoro 角を曲がったところ around (the corner)

kaemasu 替えます v exchange (money)

kaeshimasu 返します v return

kagaku 科学 science

kagi 鍵 key; lock

kagi o kakemasu 鍵をかけます

lock up

kago かご basket (grocery store)

kai 階 floor/storey [BE]

kaichuu dentoo 懐中電灯 flashlight

kaidan 階段 stairs

kaigan 海岸 beach

kaigi 会議 meeting

kaigijoo 会議場 convention hall

kaigishitsu 会議室 meeting room

kaiin shoo 会員証 membership card

kaikan jikan 開館時間 visiting hours

kaikee 会計 n bill (of sale); cashier

kaikyoo jiin 回教寺院 mosque

kaimasu 買います v buy

kaimono 買い物 shopping

kaimono o shimasu 買い物をします v shop

kajino カジノ casino

kakarimasu かかります v cost

kakekin o haraimasu 掛け金を払います v place (a bet)

kaki masu 書きます v write

kakitome 書留 registered mail

kakunin shimasu 確認します v confirm

kamera カメラ camera

kami 紙 paper

kami 髪 hair

kamisori no ha カミソリの刃 razor

blade

kanada カナダ Canada

kanadajin カナダ人 Canadian

kanai 家内 wife (one's own)

kanashii 悲しい sad

kangei shimasu 歓迎します v
welcome

kangoshi 看護士 nurse

kankee 関係 relationship

kankin shimasu 換金します v
exchange (money)

kankiri 缶切り can opener

kankoo 観光 sightseeing

kankoo annaijo 観光案内所
tourist information office

kankoo tsuaa 観光ツアー
sightseeing tour

kankookyaku 観光客 tourist

kansen shita 感染した infected

kansetsu 関節 joint (body part)

kansetsuen 関節炎 arthritis

kansha shimasu 感謝します v
thank

kanyuu shimasu 加入します v join

kanzee 関税 duty (tax)

kanzen saabisu 完全サービス full-
service

kanzoo 肝臓 liver (body part)

kanzume 缶詰 canned

kao 顔 face

kappu カップ cup

kara ni shimasu 空にします v
empty

karafu カラフ carafe

karai 辛い hot (spicy)

karimasu 借ります v rent

karorii カロリー calories

kasa 傘 umbrella

kata 肩 shoulder

katai 硬い tough **(food)**

katamichi 片道 one-way **(ticket)**

katee yoohin 家庭用品 household
good

katto カット v cut (hair)

kawa 川 river

kawa 皮 leather

kawaii 可愛い cute

kawasereeto 為替レート
exchange rate

kaze 風邪 cold (sickness)

kazoku 家族 family

keebajoo 競馬場 racetrack

keebi 警備 security

keeburu kaa ケーブル・カー cable
car

keekiya ケーキ屋 pastry shop

keeryoo kappu 計量カップ
measuring cup

keeryoo supuun 計量スプーン
measuring spoon

keesatsu 警察 police

keesatsu no shoomeesho 警察の

証明書 police report

keesu ケース case (amount)

keetai denwa 携帯電話 cell phone/
mobile phone [BE]

kekkon shimasu 結婚します v
marry

kekkon shiteiru 結婚している
married

kemikaru toire ケミカルトイレ
chemical toilet

kenkoo 健康 health

kenkoo shokuhinten 健康食品店
health food store

keshi masu 消します turn off
(lights)

keshooshitsu 化粧室 restroom/
toilet [BE]

ketsuatsu 血圧 blood pressure

ketsueki 血液 blood

ki 木 tree

kichoona 貴重な valuable

kigoo 記号 symbol (keyboard)

kigu 器具 utensil

kii horudaa キーホルダー key ring

kii kaado キーカード

kiiro 黄色 yellow

kikan 期間 period (of time)

kimasu 来ます v come

kin 金 gold

kin-en 禁煙 non-smoking

kinenkan 記念館 memorial (place)

kinko 金庫 safe (thing)

kinkyuu 緊急 emergent

kinniku 筋肉 muscle

kinoo 昨日 yesterday

kinshi shimasu 禁止します v
prohibit

kinshi 近視 near-sighted/short-
sighted [BE]

kinu 絹 silk

kinyuu shimasu 記入します v fill
out (form)

kinyuu shite kudasai 記入してくだ
さい please fill out (form)

kiosuku キオスク newsstand

kippu 切符 ticket

kippu uriba 切符売り場 ticket office

kiree きれい clean; beautiful

kiro(guramu) キロ(グラム)
kilogram

kiro(meetoru) キロ(メート
ル) kilometer

kissaten 喫茶店 café/teahouse

kisu shimasu キスします v kiss

kita 北 north

kitanai 汚い dirty

kitsuenseki 喫煙席 smoking (area)

kitte 切手 n stamp (postage)

kizu 傷 n cut

kizugusuri 傷薬 antiseptic cream

kodomo 子供 child

kodomoyoo no isu 子供用の椅子

child's seat

kodomoyoo no menyuu 子供用の
メニュー children's menu

kodomoyoo puuru 子供用プール
kiddie pool/paddling pool [BE]

koin randorii コインランドリー
laundromat/launderette [BE]

koin rokkaa コインロッカー
luggage locker

koko ここ here

kokunai no 国内の domestic

kokunaisen 国内線 domestic flight

kokusai 国際 international (airport
area)

kokusaisen 国際線 international
flight

kokuseki 国籍 nationality

kokyuu shimasu 呼吸します v
breathe

...komi ...込み with ...(included)

konban 今晩 tonight

konbanwa 今晩は good evening

konbeyaa beruto コンベヤーベル
ト conveyor belt

kondishonaa コンディショナー
conditioner

kondoomu コンドーム condom

konnichiwa こんにちは hello; good
afternoon

konpyuuta コンピュータ computer

konro コンロ stove

konsaato コンサート concert

konsaato hooru コンサートホール
concert hall

konsarutanto コンサルタント
consultant

konsento コンセント electric outlet

kontakuto renzu コンタクトレンズ
contact lens

kontakuto renzu eki コンタクトレン
ズ液 contact lens solution

konzatsu 混雑 congestion

kooban 交番 police station

karai 辛い spicy

kooen 公園 n park/playground

kooka 硬貨 coin

kookanjo 交換所 exchange (place)

kookuu gaisha 航空会社 airline

kookuubin 航空便 airmail

kookyoo 公共 public

kooreesha 高齢者 senior citizen

koori 氷 ice

kooryoku fuyoo 抗力浮揚 drag lift

koosaten 交差点 intersection

koosee busshitsu 抗生物質
antibiotic

koosha コーシャ kosher

kooshuu denwa 公衆電話 pay
phone

koosoku dooro 高速道路 highway/
motorway [BE]

koosu コース route

koosui 香水 perfume

kooto コート coat

kopii コピー photocopy

koppu コップ glass (drinking)

kore これ this

koruku sukuryuu コルクスクリュー corkscrew

koshoo 故障 breakdown

kotton コットン cotton

kottooten 骨董店 antiques store

kowaremasu 壊れます v damage

kowareta 壊れた damaged

kozutsumi 小包 package

kubi 首 neck

kuchi 口 mouth

kuchibiru 唇 lip

kujoo 苦情 complaint

kuni bangoo 国番号 country code

kurabu クラブ club

kurai 暗い dark

kurashikku ongaku クラシック音楽 classical music

kurasu クラス class

kurejitto kaado クレジットカード credit card

kuriiningu yoohin クリーニング用品 cleaning supplies

kuroi 黒い black

kuruma 車 car

kuruma isu 車椅子 wheelchair

kuruma isu yoo suroopu 車椅子用 スロープ wheelchair ramp

kuruu nekku クルーネック crew neck

kushi 櫛 comb

kusuri 薬 medicine

kutsu 靴 shoes

kutsushita 靴下 sock

kutsuya 靴屋 shoe store

kuukoo 空港 airport

kyabin キャビン cabin

kyakushitsu seesoo saabisu 客室清掃サービス housekeeping services

kyandee キャンデー candy/sweets [BE]

kyanpu kinshi キャンプ禁止 no camping

kyanpu shimasu キャンプします v camp

kyanpujoo キャンプ場 campsite

kyanseru shimasu キャンセルします v cancel

kyasshingu saabisu キャッシング・サービス cash advance

kyasshu kaado キャッシュカード ATM card

kyohi shimasu 拒否します v decline (credit card)

kyoka shimasu 許可します v permit

kyoo 今日 today

kyookai 教会 church

kyori 距離 mileage

kyuuden 宮殿 palace

kyuuka 休暇 vacation/holiday [BE]

kyuushamen 急斜面 steep

kyuukyuusha 救急車 ambulance

kyuumee booto 救命ボート life
boat

kyuumee dooi 救命胴衣 life jacket

M

maaketto マーケット market

machi 町 town

machi jikan 待ち時間 n wait

machi no hiroba 町の広場 town
square

machiaishitsu 待合室 waiting room

machiawasemasu 待ち合わせます
v meet (someone)

machigai 間違い mistake

machimasu 待ちます v wait

mado 窓 window

madogawa 窓側 window (on flight)

madogiwa 窓際 by the window

mae 前 before

maekin 前金 deposit (security)

mago 孫 grandchild

maishuu 毎週 weekly

majimena 真面目な serious

makura 枕 pillow

manikyua マニキュア manicure

manshon マンション apartment

mantan ni shimasu 満タンにします
v fill up (gasoline)

manyuaru マニュアル manual car

massaaji マッサージ massage

massugu 真っ直ぐ straight

masui 麻酔 anesthesia

maunten baiku マウンテンバイク
mountain bike

mayonaka 真夜中 midnight

me 目 eye

meeru o okurimasu メールを送りま
す v text (send a message)

meeru shimasu メールします v
e-mail

meeru メール n text (message)

meesaisho 明細書 itemized bill

meeshi 名刺 business card

megane 眼鏡 glasses

meganeten 眼鏡店 optician

memai ga shimasu めまいがしま
す dizzy

memorii kaado メモリーカード
memory card

men 綿 cotton

menyuu メニュー menu

menzee 免税 duty-free

messeeji メッセージ message

mibun shoomee 身分証明
identification

michi ni mayoi mashita 道に迷い
ました lost

michi 道 trail

midori 緑 green

migi 右 right (direction)

miharashidai 見晴し台 overlook (scenic place)

mihon 見本 specimen

mijikai 短い short

mimasu 見ます v see

mimasu 見ます v look

mimi 耳 ear

mimi ga kikoenai 耳が聞こえない deaf

mimi no itami 耳の痛み earache

minami 南 south

mini baa ミニバー mini-bar

minikui みにくい ugly

miruku ミルク milk (baby)

miryokuteki 魅力的 attractive

misa ミサ mass (church service)

misemasu 見せます v show

mizu 水 water

mizugi 水着 swimsuit

mizuumi 湖 lake

mochikomemasu 持ち込めます v allowed (on flight)

momo 腿 thigh

mondai 問題 problem

moo ichido iimasu もう一度言います v repeat

moochoo 盲腸 appendix (body part)

moodoo ken 盲導犬 guide dog

moofu 毛布 blanket

mooningu kooru モーニングコール wake-up call

mootaa booto モーターボート motor boat

mopetto モペット moped

moppu モップ mop

mori 森 forest

moshi moshi もしもし hello (on the phone)

motto もっと more

motto chiisai もっと小さい smaller

motto ii もっといい better

motto ookii もっと大きい bigger

motto ookii koe de もっと大きい声で louder

motto sukunai もっと少ない less

motto yasui もっと安い cheaper

motto yukkuri もっとゆっくり slower

muen 無鉛 unleaded (gas)

mujinno 無人の unattended

mukai 向かい opposite

mune 胸 chest (body part)

mune no itami 胸の痛み chest pain

mura 村 village

murasaki 紫 purple

muryoo 無料 free

mushi sasare 虫さされ insect bite

mushi yoke 虫除け insect repellent

mushi 虫 bug

mushiboo 無脂肪 fat free
mushiki 蒸し器 steamer
muuusu ムース mousse (hair)
muzukashii 難しい difficult

N

nabe 鍋 saucepan
nagai 長い long
nagashi 流し sink
nagasode 長袖 long sleeves
naifu ナイフ knife
naisen 内線 extension (phone)
naito kurabu ナイトクラブ nightclub
nakushimasu なくします v lose (something)
namae 名前 name
nandemo 何でも anything
nani 何 what
nankoo 軟膏 cream (ointment)
naosemasu 直せます can fix (clothing)
naoshi masu 直します v alter (clothing)/fix
napukin ナプキン napkin
nashide 無しで without
nebukuro 寝袋 sleeping bag
nedan 値段 price/value
neeru fairu ネイルファイル nail file
neeru saron ネイルサロン nail salon

nekkuresu ネックレス necklace
nekutai ネクタイ tie (clothing)
nemuke 眠気 drowsiness
nemurimasu 眠ります v sleep
nenree 年齢 age
nenza 捻挫 sprain
netsu 熱 fever; heat
nihongo 日本語 Japanese (language)
nihonjin 日本人 Japanese (people)
nikuya 肉屋 butcher
nimotsu 荷物 luggage/baggage [BE]
nimotsu hikikae ken 荷物引換券 luggage ticket
nimotsu hikikaeshoo 荷物引換証 baggage ticket
ningyoo 人形 doll
ninshin 妊娠 pregnant
nishi 西 west
nisshabyoo 日射病 sunstroke
nitsuki につき per
no tame ni のために for
nodo 喉 throat
nodo ga kawaki mashita 喉が渇きました thirsty
nodo no itami 喉の痛み sore throat
nomikomimasu 呑み込みます v swallow
nomimasu 飲みます v drink; take (medicine)

nomimono 飲み物 drink
non arukooru ノンアルコール non-alcoholic
nooka 農家 farm
norikae masu 乗り換えます v transfer (train/flight)
norimono yoi 乗物酔い motion sickness
nugimasu 脱ぎます take off (shoes)
nukimasu 抜きます v extract (tooth)
nusumaremashita 盗まれました robbed
nusumareta 盗まれた stolen
nusumimasu 盗みます v rob
nyuukoku tetsuzuki 入国手続き passport control
nyuuryoku shimasu 入力します v enter (computer)
nyuutoo futaishoo 乳糖不耐症 lactose intolerant

O

obaasan おばあさん grandmother (someone else's)
ocha お茶 tea
odorimasu 踊ります v dance
odoroku hodono 驚くほどの stunning
ofisu オフィス office
ofisu awaa オフィスアワー office hours

ogawa 小川 stream
ohashi おはし chopsticks
ohayoo gozaimasu お早うございます good morning
oiru オイル oil
oishii おいしい delicious
ojiisan おじいさん grand-father (someone else's)
oka 丘 hill
okaasan お母さん mother (some one else's)
okane お金 money
okanjoo お勘定 check (payment)
okoshimasu 起こします v wake
okugai puuru 屋外プール outdoor pool
okuremasu 遅れます v delay
okurimasu 送ります v send (mail)
okurimono 贈り物 gift
okusan 奥さん wife (someone else's)
omise kudasai お見せください v show (me)
omiyage お土産 souvenir
omiyageya お土産屋 souvenir store
omocha 玩具 toy
omochaya 玩具屋 toy store
omoshiroi 面白い interesting
omutsu o kaemasu おむつを替えます v change (baby)
omutsu おむつ diaper/nappy [BE]
onaka ga sukimashita お腹がすき

ました hungry

oneesan お姉さん sister (someone else's older)

onegai shimasu お願いします please (asking for a favor)

ongaku 音楽 music

onna no ko 女の子 girl

oniisan お兄さん brother (someone else's older)

onsen 温泉 hot spring; spa

oodekoron オーデコロン cologne

oofuku 往復 n round-trip/return [BE]

ookee オーケー OK

ookesutora オーケストラ orchestra

ookii 大きい large

oosutorariajin オーストラリア人 Australian

ootobai オートバイ motorcycle

ootomachikku オートマチック automatic car

opera hausu オペラハウス opera house

opera オペラ opera

ore 俺 I (male, informal)

oremasu 折れます v break (tooth)

orenji iro オレンジ色 orange (color)

orimasu 下ります get off (train/bus/ subway)

oritatami beddo 折り畳みベッド cot

osatsu お札 bill/note [BE]

oshaburi おしゃぶり pacifier/soother [BE]

oshiete kudasai 教えてください v show (tell me)

oshimasu 押します v push

oshiri お尻 buttocks

oshirifuki おしりふき baby wipe

oshiro お城 castle

osoi 遅い late (time)

osoimasu 襲います v mug (attack)

osoroshii 恐ろしい terrible

osusume desu お薦めです I recommend…

otera お寺 temple (religious)

otoko no ko 男の子 boy

otoko no hito 男の人 man

otoosan お父さん father (someone else's)

otooto 弟 brother (my younger)

ootosan 弟さん brother (someone else's younger)

otozuremasu 訪れます v visit

otsumami おつまみ appetizer

otsuri お釣り change (money)

otto to shibetsu shita 夫と死別した widowed

owarimasu 終わります v end

oyogimasu 泳ぎます v swim

oyu お湯 hot water

P

paato taimu パートタイム　part-time

pajama パジャマ　pajamas

pansuto パンスト　pantyhose/tights [BE]

pantii パンティー　briefs (clothing)

pantsu パンツ　underwear/underpants [BE]

pan-ya パン屋　bakery

pasu waado パスワード　password

pasupooto パスポート　passport

pedikyua ペディキュア　pedicure

peepaa taoru ペーパータオル　paper towel

pen ペン　pen

penishirin ペニシリン　penicillin

penisu ペニス　penis

petiito ペティート　petite

pikunikkujoo ピクニック場　picnic area

pinku ピンク　pink

piru ピル　Pill (birth control)

piza resutoran ピザ・レストラン　pizzeria

poketto ポケット　pocket

pondo ポンド　pound (British sterling)

pondo ポンド　pound (weight)

popyuraa ongaku ポピュラー音楽　pop music

pun 分　minute

purachina プラチナ　platinum

purasu saizu プラス サイズ　plus size

purinto shimasu プリントします　v print

puripeedo keetai プリペイド携帯　prepaid phone

puuru プール　pool

R

raifu gaado ライフガード　lifeguard

raitaa ライター　lighter

raketto ラケット　racket (sports)

randorii saabisu ランドリーサービス　laundry service

rappu ラップ　plastic wrap/cling film [BE]

rappu ラップ　rap (music)

rasshu ラッシュ　rush

ree 零　zero

reenkooto レーンコート　raincoat

reesu レース　lace

reeto レート　exchange rate

reetooko 冷凍庫　freezer

reezooko 冷蔵庫　refrigerator

regyuraa レギュラー　regular

rekkaasha レッカー車　tow truck

renraku 連絡　connection (flight)

rentakaa レンタカー　rental car/hire car BE]

renzu レンズ　lens

reshiito レシート　receipt

ressha 列車　train

ressun レッスン　lesson

resutoran レストラン　restaurant

rifuto リフト　lift

rifutoken リフト券　lift pass

rikon shimasu 離婚します　v divorce

ringu リング　ring

rinsu リンス　conditioner

rippa 立派　magnificent

risaikuringu リサイクリング　recycling

rittoru リットル　liter

riyoo shimasu 利用します　v utilize

roguofu shimasu ログオフします　log off

roguon shimasu ログオンします　log on

rokkaa ロッカー　locker

rokkotsu 肋骨　rib (body part)

romanchikku ロマンチック　romantic

roofaa ローファー　loafers

rooshon ローション　lotion

rosen 路線　track (train)

ruumu saabisu ルームサービス　room service

ryokan 旅館　inn

ryokoo dairiten 旅行代理店　travel agency

ryokoo 旅行　trip

ryoo 寮　dormitory

ryoogae 両替　currency exchange

ryoogae shimasu 両替します　v exchange (money)

ryoogaejo 両替所　currency exchange office

ryoojikan 領事館　consulate

ryookin meetaa 料金メーター　parking meter

ryookin 料金　charge (cost)

ryoori shimasu 料理します　v cook

ryooshuusho 領収書　receipt

ryukkusakku リュックサック　backpack

ryuugakuseeshoo 留学生証　international student card

S

saabisu サービス　service (in a restaurant)

saafu boodo サーフボード　surfboard

sabaku 砂漠　desert

saifu 財布　purse; wallet

saigo 最後　last

saikuringu サイクリング　cycling

sainshimasu サインします　v sign

saisho no 最初の　first

saizu サイズ　size

sakana 魚　fish

sakaya 酒屋　liquor store/off-licence

[BE]

sakkaa サッカー soccer

sakkaa geemu サッカーゲーム soccer/football [BE] game

sakujo shimasu 削除します v delete

samui 寒い cold (weather)

sandaru サンダル sandals

sangurasu サングラス sunglasses

sanpo 散歩 n walk

sanpomichi 散歩道 walking route

sanshoo 山頂 peak (of a mountain)

sanso chiryoo 酸素治療 oxygen treatment

sara 皿 plate

sauna サウナ sauna

sayoonara さようなら goodbye

seebyoo 性病 sexually transmitted disease (STD)

seekyuu shimasu 請求します v bill (charge)

seekyuusho 請求書 invoice

seeri 生理 period (menstrual)

seeriyoo napukin 生理用ナプキン sanitary napkin/pad [BE]

seetaa セーター sweater

seiritsuu 生理痛 menstrual cramp

seki 咳 cough

seki 席 seat

sekitsui 脊椎 spine (body part)

sekken 石鹸 soap

seminaa セミナー seminar

sen 線 line (train)

senaka 背中 back (body part)

senchi meetoru センチメートル centimeter

senjooato 戦場跡 battleground

senjoozai 洗浄剤 cleaning product

senmon-i 専門医 specialist (doctor)

senmonka 専門家 expert (skill level)

sennuki 栓抜き bottle opener

senpuuki 扇風機 fan (appliance)

sensui yoogu 潜水用具 diving equipment

sentaku 洗濯 laundry

sentaku shisetsu 洗濯施設 laundry facility

sentakuki 洗濯機 washing machine

senzai 洗剤 detergent

serufu saabisu セルフサービス self-service

sesshi 摂氏 Celsius

setomono 瀬戸物 china

setsuzoku 接続 connection (internet)

setsuzoku o kirimasu 接続を切ります disconnect (computer)

setsuzoku shimasu 接続します v connect (internet)

shanpuu シャンプー shampoo

shashin 写真 photo

shashin satsuee 写真撮影
photography

shatsu シャツ shirt

shawaa シャワー shower

sheebingu kuriimu シェービングク
リーム shaving cream

shiai 試合 *n* match

shibai 芝居 *n* play (theater)

shichakushitsu 試着室 fitting room

shigai chizu 市街地図 town map

shigai kyokuban 市外局番 area
code

shigoto 仕事 business

shihainin 支配人 manager
(restaurant, hotel)

shihee 紙幣 *n* bill (money)/note [BE]

shii dii CD CD

shiitsu シーツ sheet

shikaku shoogaisha 視覚障害者
visually impaired

shikki 漆器 lacquerware

shimasu します *v* play

shimemasu 閉めます *v* close (a
shop)

shinbun 新聞 newspaper

shindai 寝台 berth

shindaisha 寝台車 sleeper car

shingoo 信号 traffic light

shinguru beddo シングルベッド
single bed

shinguru ruumu シングルルーム

single room

shinju 真珠 pearl

shinnyuu shimasu 侵入します
break-in (burglary)

shintai shoogaisha 身体障害者
disabled; handicapped

shinzoo 心臓 heart

shinzoobyoo 心臓病 heart
condition

shirabemasu 調べます *v* check
(something)

shirasemasu 知らせます *v* notify

shiroi 白い white

shisnkoku shimasu 申告します *v*
declare

shita 舌 tongue

shitagi 下着 underwear

shitsu 質 quality

shitsumon 質問 question

shitsunai puuru 室内プール
indoor pool

shitsuree shimasu 失礼しま
す excuse me (to get past)

shiyakusho 市役所 town hall

shizen hogoku 自然保護区 nature
preserve

shizuka 静か quiet

shohoo shimasu 処方します
v prescribe

shohoosen 処方箋 prescription

shohoosen nashi 処方箋無し over

the counter (medication)

shokki 食器 dish (kitchen)

shokubutsuen 植物園 botanical garden

shokudoo 食堂 dining room

shokuji 食事 meal

shokuryoohin 食料品 produce

shokuryoohinten 食料品店 grocery store

shokusen ki 食洗機 dishwasher

shomeeshimasu 署名します *v* sign

shooboosho 消防署 fire department

shoogo 正午 noon

shoohizee 消費税 sales tax

shoojoo 症状 condition (medical)

shookai shimasu 紹介します *v* introduce

shookeesu ショーケース display case

shookyo shimasu 消去します *v* clear (on an ATM)

shoonikai 小児科医 pediatrician

shooten gai 商店街 shopping area

shoppingu mooru ショッピングモール shopping mall

shoshinsha 初心者 novice (skill level)

shujin 主人 husband (one's own)

shukketsu shimasu 出血します *v* bleed

shukuboo 宿坊 temple accommodation

shukuhaku setsubi 宿泊設備 accommodation

shuppatsu 出発 departure

shusseki shimasu 出席します *v* attend

shuu 週 week

shuuji yoogu 習字用具 calligraphy supplies

shuumatsu 週末 weekend

shuuri shimasu 修理します *v* repair

shuurikoo 修理工 mechanic

shuurikoojoo 修理工場 garage

sobo 祖母 grandmather (one's own)

sofu 祖父 grandfather (one's own)

sofubo 祖父母 grandparents (one's own)

soko そこ there

sokutatsu 速達 express

sookin shimasu 送金します *v* transfer (money)

soonyuu shimasu 挿入します *v* insert (on an ATM)

soto 外 outside

…sugimasu …過ぎます too…

sugoi すごい amazing

suihanki 炊飯器 rice cooker

suijoo sukii 水上スキー water skis

suisen shimasu 推薦します *v* recommend

suisen 推薦 recommendation

suishoo 水晶 crystal

sukaafu スカーフ scarf

sukaato スカート skirt

sukidesu 好きです *v* like

sukii スキー ski

sukii rifuto スキーリフト chair lift

sukoshi 少し little

sukyanaa スキャナー scanner

sumi 炭 charcoal

sumimasen すみません excuse me (apology)

sumimasu 住みます *v* live

sunakku baa スナックバー snack bar

suniikaa スニーカー sneaker

sunoo boodo スノーボード snowboard

sunookeru yoogu スノーケル用具 snorkeling equipment

supiido ihan スピード違反 speeding

supootsu スポーツ sports

supootsu yoohinten スポーツ用品店 sporting goods store

supuun スプーン spoon

suriipingu baggu スリーピングバッグ sleeping bag

surippa スリッパ slippers

surudoi 鋭い sharp

sushi ya 寿司屋 sushi restaurant

sutaato shimasu スタートします *v* start (a car)

sutajiamu スタジアム stadium

suteki すてき nice

sutokku ストック poles (skiing)

suuji 数字 number

suupaa スーパー super (fuel)

suupaa スーパー supermarket

suutsu スーツ suit

suutsu keesu スーツケース suitcase

suwarimasu 座ります *v* sit

suzushii 涼しい cool (temperature)

T

taaminaru ターミナル terminal (airport)

tabako 煙草 cigarette

tabako o suimasu 煙草を吸います *v* smoke

tabakoya 煙草屋 tobacconist

tabeamasu 食べます *v* eat

tabemono 食物 food

tachiiri kinshi 立入禁止 no access

tada ただ only

taika tobira 耐火扉 fire door

taipu shimasu タイプします *v* type

taishoku shita 退職した retired

taiya タイヤ tire/tyre [BE]

taiyoo 太陽 sun

takai 高い expensive; high

taki 滝 waterfall

takibi kinshi 焚火禁止 no fires

takushii タクシー taxi

tanima 谷間 valley

tanjoobi 誕生日 birthday

tanoshii 楽しい happy

tanoshimi 楽しみ pleasure

tanoshimimasu 楽しみます ∨ enjoy

tanpon タンポン tampon

taoru タオル towel

tasuke 助け help

tasukete 助けて help me!

tatemono 建物 building

te 手 hand

teeburu テーブル table

omochikaeri お持ち帰り take-out/ take away [BE]

tegami 手紙 letter/post [BE]

tekubi 手首 wrist

tenchoo 店長 manager (shop)

tenimotsu 手荷物 carry-on/hand luggage [BE]

tenimotsu hikiwatashijo 手荷物引 渡所 baggage claim

tenisu テニス tennis

tenki 天気 weather

tennai no annai 店内の案内 store directory

tento テント tent

tento no shichuu テントの支 柱 tent pole

tento yoo pegu テント用ペグ tent peg

terakotta テラコッタ terracotta

terebi テレビ TV

terehon kaado テレホンカード **phone** card

tii shatsu Tシャツ T-shirt

tisshu peepaa ティッシュペーパ ー tissue

tobikomimasu 飛び込みます ∨ dive

todokimasu 届きます ∨ reach

toire トイレ bathroom (toilet)

toire no kyuuingu トイレの吸引 具 plunger

toiretto peepaa トイレットペーパ ー toilet paper

tokoya 床屋 barber

tokubetsuna 特別な extra

tokudai 特大 extra large

tomarimasu 止まります ∨ stop

tomarimasu 泊まります ∨ stay (overnight)

too 塔 tower

toochaku 到着 arrivals (airport)

tooi 遠い far

toojoo ken 搭乗券 boarding pass

toojoo shimasu 搭乗します ∨ board (plane)

tooki 陶器 pottery

toonan 盗難 theft

toonyoobyoo 糖尿病 diabetic

tooza yokin 当座預金 checking account/current account [BE]

tooza yoking kooza 当座預金口座 checking account

toraberaazu chekku トラベラーズチェック traveler's check/traveller's cheque [BE]

toreenaa トレーナー sweatshirt

toreeningu jimu トレーニングジム gym

tori 鳥 bird

torikaemasu 取り替えます v exchange (goods)

torimu トリム trim (hair cut)

toshi 年 year

toshiyori 年寄り old (person)

toshokan 図書館 library

tsuaa ツアー tour

tsugi 次 next

tsukaemasen 使えません doesn't work

tsukaimasu 使います v use

tsukaisute 使い捨て disposable

tsukaisute kamisori 使い捨カミソリ disposable razor

tsukare mashita 疲れました tired

tsukareta 疲れた exhausted

tsukemasu つけます turn on (lights)

tsukeawase 付け合わせ side dish

tsukimasu 着きます v arrive

tsuki 月 month

tsuki 付き with… (attached)

tsumaranai つまらない boring

tsume 爪 fingernail

tsumemasu 詰めます v pack

tsumemono 詰物 filling (tooth)

tsumetai 冷たい cold (food)

tsuretekimasu 連れてきます v bring

tsutsumimasu 包みます v wrap (a package)

tsuuka 通貨 currency

tsuuro 通路 aisle

tsuurogawa no zaseki 通路側の座席 aisle seat

tsuuyakusha 通訳者 interpreter

tsuzuri o iimasu つづりを言います v spell

U

ude dokee 腕時計 watch

ude 腕 arm

ueetaa ウェーター waiter

ueetoresu ウェートレス waitress

ueno 上の upper

uketorimasu 受け取ります v pick up (something)

uketsuke 受付 reception

umi 海 sea

unten menkyoshoo 運転免許証 driver's license

unten menkyoshoo bangoo 運転免許証番号 driver's license number

unten shimasu 運転します v drive

urimasu 売ります v sell

urin 雨林 rainforest

ushiro 後ろ behind (direction)

utsukushii 美しい beautiful

uuru ウール wool

W

waiaresu intaanetto ワイアレスインターネット wireless internet

waiaresu intaanetto saabisu ワイアレスインターネットサービス wireless internet service

wain risuto ワインリスト wine list

wakai 若い young

wakarimasen 分かりません I don't understand

wakarimasu 分かります v understand

wanpiisu ワンピース dress (piece of clothing)

waribiki 割引 discount

watakushi 私 I (formal)

Y

yakemasu 焼けます v burn

yakisugi 焼き過ぎ overdone

yakkyoku 薬局 pharmacy/chemist [BE]

yakyuu 野球 baseball

yama 山 mountain

yasashii やさしい easy

yasui 安い inexpensive

yatoimasu 雇います v rent/hire [BE]

yoboo sesshu 予防接種 vaccination

yodooshi 夜通し overnight

yohoo 予報 forecast

yoku yasumi mashita よく休みました well-rested

yoofukuya 洋服屋 clothing store

yooi ga dekite iru 用意ができている ready

yooshi 用紙 form (fill-in)

yoru 夜 night

yotee 予定 n schedule

yotee ni iremasu 予定に入れます v schedule

yoyaku madoguchi 予約窓口 reservation desk

yoyaku shimasu 予約します v reserve

yoyaku 予約 appointment; reservation

yubi 指 finger

yubiwa 指輪 ring

yuki no ooi 雪の多い snowy

yukigutsu 雪靴 snowshoe

yukkuri ゆっくり slowly